More Praise for This Book

"Use the concise and engaging information in Clark Quinn's new book to move beyond the myths, fads, and folklore that hold us and our organizations back. One of the best benefits is learning how to analyze others' learning, training, and outcomes claims. So important."

—Patti Shank
Author, *Write and Organize for Deeper Learning*
and *Practice and Feedback for Deeper Learning*

"This book is useful for those who want or need to investigate the truth behind learning myths, superstitions, and misconceptions. The clear structure, short sections, and solid research make it a worthy addition for anyone who cares about learning."

—Mirjam Neelen
Learning Advisory Manager

"*Millennials, Goldfish & Other Training Misconceptions* is a tremendous contribution to assist in the necessary move toward evidence-based practice for L&D practitioners and their clients. Clark Quinn not only addresses the prevailing myths, superstitions, and misconceptions in the field today with what the research says, but also provides excellent guidance for what to do instead."

—Guy Wallace
President, EPPIC

"Clark Quinn has provided an invaluable service to our profession with this incredibly useful book. He's not only explained the issues with numerous myths and beliefs, but also takes the time to give us suggestions about what we can do to make better learning experiences. It's an essential book for any conscientious practitioner."

—Julie Dirksen
Author, *Design for How People Learn*

MILLENNIALS, GOLDFISH & OTHER TRAINING MISCONCEPTIONS

DEBUNKING LEARNING MYTHS AND SUPERSTITIONS

CLARK N. QUINN

PRESS

ATD Press is an internationally renowned source of insightful and practical information on
talent development, training, and professional development.

ATD Press
1640 King Street
Alexandria, VA 22314 USA

Ordering information: Books published by ATD Press can be purchased by visiting ATD's
website at www.td.org/books or by calling 800.628.2783 or 703.683.8100.

Library of Congress Control Number: 2018935628

ISBN-10: 1-947308-37-8
ISBN-13: 978-1-947308-37-4
e-ISBN: 978-1-947308-38-1

ATD Press Editorial Staff
Director: Kristine Luecker
Manager: Melissa Jones
Community of Practice Manager, Learning Technologies: Justin Brusino
Developmental Editor: Jack Harlow
Text and Cover Design: Francelyn Fernandez
Printed by Versa Press Inc., East Peoria, IL

To all who fight the good fight
for science and improvement in
the human condition.

CONTENTS

THE MYTHS, SUPERSTITIONS, AND MISCONCEPTIONS

FOREWORD

Clark Stanley worked as a cowboy and later as a very successful entrepreneur, selling medicine in the United States that he made based on secrets he learned from an Arizona Hopi Indian medicine man. His elixir was made from rattlesnake oil, and was marketed in the 1890s through public events in which Stanley killed live rattlesnakes and squeezed out their oil in front of admiring crowds. After his medicine gained a wide popularity, he was able to set up production facilities in Massachusetts and Rhode Island with the help of a pharmacist. Stanley made himself a rich man.

You may not know his name, but you've certainly heard of Stanley's time and place. It was the era of patent medicines—false and sometimes dangerous elixirs sold to men and women of all stripes: Dr. Kilmer's Swamp Root. Oxien. Kickapoo Indian Sagwa. Dr. Morse's Indian Root Pills. Enzyte. Bonnore's Electro Magnetic Bathing Fluid. Radithor. Liquozone. And of course, Clark Stanley's Snake Oil Liniment.

These medicines were bought by the millions. Fortunes were made. And millions of people were bamboozled, sickened, or even killed.

Upon being tested, Stanley's elixir was found to be made mostly from mineral oil—a worthless potion sold by a charlatan. His story of the medicine man and the rattlesnake juice was a more potent concoction than his famous elixir.

So what causes men and women to miss the truth, to fail to see, and to continue happily in harming themselves and those around them? This, unfortunately, is not a question just for the era of patent medicines. It is eternal. It goes back to the dawn of humanity and continues today. I have no answer except to assume that our credulity is part of our humanity—and should guide us to be on guard at all times.

What stopped the patent-medicine pandemic of poison, persuasion, and placebo? Did we rise up and throw out the scoundrels, the money-grubbers, the snake-oil salesmen? Did we see that we were deceived because we were too hopeful or too blind? Did we heed our senses and find a way to overcome the hidden dangers? No! We did not!

It was not a mass movement back to rationality and truth that saved us. It was the work of a few intrepid journalists, who began reporting on the deaths, sicknesses, and addictions resulting from the use of patent medicines. In 1905, *Collier's Weekly* published a cover story that exploded the industry: "The Great American Fraud: The Patent Medicine Evil," written by former crime reporter Samuel Hopkins Adams.

This long piece of investigative journalism opened the floodgates and led directly to the Pure Food and Drug Act in 1906. The act was followed by additional regulations and requirements that protect our health and safety.

The ugly truth is that we need help in seeing what we can't or won't see. This is also true in the learning industry, and has been since at least the early 1900s. When I decided to start Work-Learning Research to bridge the gap between research and practice, it was because I kept seeing bogus recommendations steal attention away from more fundamental and effective learning practices. And, about 20 years later, the proverbial snake oil continues to vex our field and push us to make poor decisions about learning.

Alas, I am a faint voice in the howling wind of our industry. Fortunately, there are many other muckraking practitioners today, including folks like Paul Kirschner, Patti Shank, Guy Wallace, Pedro De Bruyckere, Julie Dirksen, Donald Clark, Ruth Clark, Mirjam Neelen, and Jane Bozarth. There are also legions of academic researchers who do the science necessary to enable us to convey research-to-practice wisdom to trainers, instructional designers, e-learning developers, and learning executives.

I am especially optimistic now that Clark Quinn has compiled the myths, superstitions, and misconceptions that imbue our field with faulty decision making and ineffective learning practices. As Clark rightly advises, don't read the book in one sitting. You will find it too much to think that our field could tolerate so much snake oil.

But here's what many don't realize. Blindly going along with today's workplace learning fads costs the industry billions of dollars in wasted effort, misspent resources, and ill-advised decisions. They distract us from the fundamentals of the science of learning that have proven to be effective! Every time trainers read an article on learning styles and adjust their training programs to make them suitable for visual, auditory, kinesthetic, and olfactory learners. Every time instructional designers attend a conference session touting that neuroscience can replace all other learning design, and then scrap their other learning strategies. Every time a chief learning officer hears that all learning events, no matter their content or purpose, should be shrunk to four-minute microlearning videos—that storytelling is everything, that all learning is social, that virtual reality is the future of learning. Every time our learning executives jump on a bandwagon, we open ourselves up to ignoring what really works.

Let us start anew today. We can begin with Clark's book; it is a veritable treasure chest of wisdom. But let's keep going. Let's stay skeptical. Let's look to the scientific research for knowledge. Let's become more demanding and knowledgeable ourselves, knowing that we all have more to learn. Let's do our own testing. Let's improve our evaluation systems so that we get better feedback day by day. Let's pilot, rework, improve, and continue to learn!

As the history of patent medicine shows, we must be forever vigilant against our blindness and against those who will sell us the miraculous hope of the next workplace cure-alls.

—Will Thalheimer, PhD
President of Work-Learning Research
Somerville, Massachusetts
April 2018

PREFACE

Why This Book

Many myths, despite publicity about their invalidity, still persist in instructional design practices. Beliefs about learners and learning that don't reflect what is known from science continue to exist. It can be costly when we invest resources in developing programs to accommodate them, and they undermine the learning outcomes we're trying to achieve.

In this book, I lay out the myths that affect adult learning in the organization. They're broken up into three categories:

- myths that research has shown are not valid (such as learning styles)
- design practices that are prevalent but aren't backed up by science (such as smile sheets)
- common approaches or beliefs that have been misconstrued and need clarification (including 70-20-10).

Each of these has implications for practice. When we practice in alignment with what is known, our learning approaches are scrutable. When our designs violate learning science prescriptions, we are wasting resources *and* wasting our learners' time.

Whom This Book Is For

This book is for those in organizational learning, whether internal-facing or external learning experiences. You may be at the individual instructional designer, manager, or executive level, but this book is for anyone who makes decisions about how learning is designed and delivered.

Beyond the instructional designer level, this book is for those responsible for learning policies, procedures, and processes: those who determine how learning *should* be applied. Those who manage or control the process. And those who lead those managers and teams. Practitioners in these roles should be aware of what learning science says—and work in alignment with these practices.

If you are responsible for the design of learning experiences, you should have a copy of this book and be aware of the contents. Ultimately, *you* are the one who needs to commit to learning that withstands any challenges on the quality of the outcome. While cost and speed are understandable concerns, learning that doesn't work is ultimately a waste of time *and* money.

How to Read It

This book is *not* meant to be read from front to back. While that's not a bad idea, the intention is for you to use it as a guide to those issues you face. It's for you to use when confronted with viewpoints contrary to good practices or when facing contention around controversial proposals. Use it to make a case for good learning design!

I strongly encourage you to read the first two chapters, particularly the one on the science of learning. They provide essential background information as well as a foundation for much of the subsequent explanations.

I urge you to look at the table of contents or page through the book, and check out the topics you are curious about. Maybe it's whether Millennials learn differently from other generations. Or maybe you're curious about the attention span of your learners. In fact, you may actually (or implicitly) be practicing some of these myths right now. An important step to correcting a myth is consciously challenging your own assumptions!

Too many situations arise when people ask for or expect designs or implementations that reflect personal beliefs, yet run contrary to what science has determined works. If you struggle to convince your peers of the value of an alternative approach, this book is designed to be your partner. Feel free to wield it as a defense!

ACKNOWLEDGMENTS

Many people through the years have provided contributions that led to this book. While I've been paying attention to learning science (and myths) for decades, the necessary focus on the problem and the need for solutions is more recent. There are many contributors, and I've no doubt missed a few. Mea culpa!

Many years ago, Chad Udell, of Float Mobile, and I did an eLearning Guild presentation on learning myths. His firm provided some excellent graphics, and we debunked a number of myths. That was sort of the gestation of a series of presentations that gradually expanded in scope.

Will Thalheimer has been a friend and colleague, and has been a standard-bearer to the extent of running the Debunker's Club and putting money behind a challenge to anyone who can show value in learning styles. I thought he should be a co-author, but he (perhaps wisely) declined on the lack of a clear business case. He has been an eager supporter of the work, and graciously agreed to write the foreword.

Patti Shank has been a sounding board several times for my work. She previously conducted research for the eLearning Guild, and since has been leading the charge at ATD's Science of Learning blog. I've written for it, and it's generally a good source on what's happening in the field. She's also started a new series of books that compile valuable design guidance.

Julie Dirksen and Michael Allen have been co-campaigners with Will and I in the Serious eLearning Manifesto (elearningmanifesto.org). While not specifically discussing myths, they've both been an inspiration for fighting for what's important. Their writings on good design are based on sound learning science.

In addition to the people named, a number of friends came through in my request for assistance in identifying myths. Jane Bozarth, Connie Malamed, Mark Britz, Karen Hyder, Bianca Woods, Sarah Gilbert, Trina Rimmer, Cammy Bean, Karl Kapp, Megan Torrance, Dave Ferguson, Cathy Moore, Maria Andersen, Steve Nguyen, Jason Haag, Brian Dusablon, Kris Rockwell, Steve Howard, Joe Ganci, Mirjam Neelen, Paul Kirschner, and Guy Wallace all offered their help. Their contributions are greatly appreciated.

Members of the Debunker's Club also responded, including Dan Topf, Margaret Driscoll, Rick Presly, Marty Rosenheck, John McDermott, Paul Kirschner, Adam Neaman, Steve Madsen, Michelle Perry-Slater, Viv Cole, Steve Villachica, Peter Mitchell, Donald H. Taylor, and Mackenzie Peterson. Their support is gratefully accepted.

At ATD, Jack Harlow served as my developmental editor and not only massaged my prose, but made contributions that significantly improved. Melissa Jones served as copy editor and coordinated the comics that accompany the descriptions. Francelyn Fernandez is responsible for the comics themselves, and did a great job interpreting my meaning. Deborah Orgel Hudson and Julia Dragel joined in to assist with marketing. It's been a pleasure to work with them, and I'm grateful to all the folks at ATD.

I owe a special thanks to Justin Brusino. He not only has involved me in a number of projects through the years, but he was the one who suggested that we do this book. He was there for me through *Revolutionize Learning & Development*, and he's been there throughout this process. He's quiet, but he has a big impact on the field. Thanks!

My children, Declan and Erin, provide a regular motivation to continue to fight for what's right. I believe it's important to model principled behavior, and they're an additional reason beyond my personal code of conduct. They make me proud.

Most important, I owe eternal gratitude to my wife, my friend, the mother of our children, and my best editor, LeAnn. She provides the emotional and physical support so I can undertake such endeavors. Thanks, dear lady.

THE MYTHS THAT HOLD US BACK

Beliefs and the State of Design

Many myths persist despite the evidence, and many of them affect the learning and training industry. Despite research results and considerable attention, large numbers of myths are still endorsed by the public (including teachers). For example, researchers have documented that even 78 percent of those with some neuroscience education believe in learning styles (Macdonald et al. 2017)! The data for teachers and the public at large are worse. Other myths have their own persistent believers.

Similarly, there are misconceptions about a variety of learning design topics that lead people to misinterpret the intent or avoid the good elements because of wariness around bad connotations. So, if we hear that a model is controversial, we might avoid it even though there are benefits to be found. If something is derided because of one interpretation but another way to view it is useful, it helps to clarify the meanings to separate out the valuable from the detrimental.

What does this mean? For one, it means that we can practice what we believe is good learning design in many ways—and end up wasting time and money. We can also squander goodwill if what we pursue ends up leading to dissatisfaction on the part of stakeholders.

If learning design is a field that aspires to be truly professional, mistaken beliefs can serve to undermine our credibility. Practitioners must be aware of what is legitimate, what is unproven, and what has been thoroughly debunked. When we follow fads instead of what learning science tells us, we can run into many problems. First, and most important, we may do bad for our learners. Second, we may waste valuable time and money; our organizations should expect better. And third, we could undermine our legitimacy, and thus continue to be seen as a cost, not an investment.

To put it another way, the learning field should be as professional as any other, and knowing what's fanciful from what's factual should be a matter of pride. We wouldn't want to be the perpetrators of learning malpractice, after all. It's not fair to those who employ us or those who depend on us.

Learning Myths

Myths, as I refer to them here, are beliefs that are prevalent despite repeated evidence that they're wrong. These learning myths cause us to invest in approaches that either waste time and money or hinder learning, which harms both the field and our learners. It's like we suddenly decided to go back to astrology instead of astronomy!

It's easy to understand the appeal of many myths—some based on tidy round numbers, others on how we'd prefer to believe people learn—so their persistence would be understandable if there wasn't a surfeit of evidence against them. They tap into our own experiences and beliefs about how the world works, but ultimately don't test out.

In this book, we consider the claim, the appeal, and the potential upsides and downsides for each myth. Then we look at the type of evidence that might illustrate whether the myth is valid. Finally, we'll unpack what the research says. So as not to leave you in the lurch, I also suggest alternate approaches you can use to get the best learning outcomes.

The aim is to provide a succinct, clear argument about why some beliefs are myths, and what to do instead. I encourage you to carry a copy of this book so you can point out the problem to those who ask you to alter your design to accommodate a myth.

Learning Superstitions

In addition to the myths just described, I want to call attention to a second category, which emerged from feedback provided by colleagues in the field. These learning superstitions are semi-myths that we see in practice, which lead to bad learning design. Not as obviously labeled "myths," they are still practices we see too often and work contrary to the best learning outcomes.

In this section, we'll look at the practice, explore the rationale behind why people might believe it, explain why it doesn't work, and dive into what to do instead. These superstitions are a source of irritation for those who proselytize good design and face continuing bad practices.

Again, the intent is for you to have a quick resource to use to counter requests that are contrary to good learning design. You may even find some of your own beliefs challenged!

Learning Misconceptions

Misconceptions are yet a different category. Here, we're not necessarily dealing with "right or wrong." Instead, this section looks at certain models that have led to contention. For each candidate, I lay out the two alternate views and propose a reconciliation. Whether you prefer to believe in the resulting viewpoint is a choice only you can make.

In these cases, some viewpoints say the concept is useful, while others say it has issues. These frameworks can provide value, but they can be misused as well. It's important for you to understand what's good and bad with each, and then choose whether the good can be leveraged to your benefit or it's too problematic.

Being a Smart Consumer

It is incumbent on us, as professionals, to be savvy about what constitutes reputable science. It helps to have a set of principles that can serve as a guide; a "sniff test" of sorts to see if the suggested result seems pure. The following heuristics—or problem-solving strategies—can provide a guide to whether there's a potential problem:

- **Proprietary studies.** When doing your due diligence in researching a topic, you may come across someone saying that *their* data say X. A good rule of thumb is to always ask if the data were published in a peer-reviewed journal. Unpublished data are suspect, because why wouldn't you publish if you could? Peer review isn't everything—it can have its own faults and loopholes—but it's a good source of scientific rigor. If the claim is that the data and the collection method are proprietary, then how can they tell you about it? Be wary of someone saying they have data that can't be shared. Proper research includes sufficient information to replicate the study and see if the same results are produced. If you're required to purchase their proprietary product or service to get the data, you have to wonder about their scrutability.
- **Who's telling you?** Similar to the above, if those who are presenting a particular approach have a vested interest in touting research that supports the approach, be wary. It's usually possible to find *some* study that portrays a particular viewpoint. And you may not be able to decipher whether the data are biased. (Sadly, there is evidence of organizations influencing data across all industries and fields; this is not unique to learning design.) Also, it's possible to pick studies that justify a position regardless of exact relevance. Which leads to . . .
- **Even or round numbers.** When claims are made with numbers that come out round, particularly multiples of 10, you should check to see whether the researchers or organization behind them are touting that the numbers are from real data or are using it as a framework. Real data tend to look messy: you'll get 6.3 percent who do this and 13.9 percent who do that. Quality research is highly unlikely to result in clean numbers (although unround numbers are no guarantee either: see 7-38-55). It's not always a good guide, and the numbers may be used as a guide instead of an exact claim (see 70-20-10), but if someone's saying you should react in exact proportions, you should be leery.

- **Overgeneralization.** Organizations can choose data that address a small fraction of what they're saying, and then generalize to support their point. A recent example I've seen conflated studies about online learning and mobile device usage to make a claim for mobile learning. In the piece, the two things were completely separate, and inferences were used to make a case for something that was at the (empty) intersection. Good research very clearly states the limits to which the data can be generalized.
- **Rival hypotheses.** In graduate school, I was trained using published studies to detect opportunities for alternative, simpler explanations. And a large proportion of studies had alternative hypotheses that couldn't be precluded. It's often the case, even with legitimate research, to create a complex explanation when a more obvious story better suits the outcome. We'll see this with the myth about generations, in which much of the behavior of a younger generation can be explained by stage of life rather than the specific circumstance of growing up. You want to make sure that the claim can't be explained in another, more plausible way.
- **Correlation does not equal causation.** If things occur together, it's easy to infer that they're related. However, that's not necessarily the case. For example, if more people die in hospitals than at home, is it because hospitals are unsafe? Or because people tend to be in the hospital because they're already unwell?
- And, of course, there's always the tried-and-true test: **If it sounds too good to be true, it probably is.**

Now that we've covered some heuristics, what should you do?

- **Look to those who bear the standard of science.** There are individuals in the learning design space who consistently strive to investigate what research tells us and translate it into practical guidance. The appendix includes a list of mythbusters, those who have demonstrated a consistent ability to make sense of the learning science. Track these people!

- **Check for consonant studies.** Don't simply accept one source—look for reinforcements! Are there multiple studies? Is there other converging evidence? Has someone replicated the results? Has the study been published in a peer-reviewed journal?
- **Does the claim pass the "sniff" test?** Our intuitions can be a powerful guide in areas we have some knowledge about. Does the story seem plausible? Under what conditions would this make sense?
- **Use causal reasoning.** You can use casual reasoning to try to see if what's being presented makes sense. Is there a mechanism that explains the result? What cognitive story makes sense here?
- **Check to see the constraints.** Under what conditions should you use the result? You should check to see what the limitations are on the implications. Are the results being extrapolated to situations that aren't representative of the initial study?

Let's be clear, none of this is foolproof. Evidence can be tainted in multiple ways. There are no guarantees. The best you can do is pursue due diligence about the sources and be skeptical. And while I'm confident in my own research, this includes what I cover in this book!

Dealing With Believers

While factual arguments usually convince open minds, there is considerable evidence that this doesn't hold in all cases. In fact, if particular beliefs are tied to an individual's values or world view, facts will actually strengthen them! This makes myths and misconceptions difficult to deal with, so here are some of my suggestions.

This book is designed to give you the ammunition you need to deal with those who might argue against the science. And, since it's not always easy to recall the necessary science, each section not only outlines the belief, but also the reason it's wrong and any other arguments that can be construed. While the sections on superstitions and misconceptions aren't always backed up by a study, each learning myth includes one. I've also created quick reference cards for each myth, superstition, and misconception. You'll find them in the back. Hopefully, that's enough.

Unfortunately, it won't always be. There are those who possess a vested interest in the myth—for instance, if they're selling an associated product—want you to believe it and will cite studies that demonstrate the validity of their claim. Unless you're well-trained in research methodology, it can be challenging to identify potential flaws in their data (although practicing being a smart consumer will help). They might suggest that "our studies have shown," or the research cited in this book is old. While that's possible, it's not likely. As suggested earlier, unless their data have been published in a peer-reviewed journal of repute, it's open to suspicion. Why wouldn't you publish something that demonstrates your superiority? Proprietary methods don't preclude statistically significant studies of impact—they just give you extra reasons to be dubious.

THE SCIENCE OF LEARNING

Decades of Research

Empirical research into the science of learning arguably started with Ebbinghaus's study of memory in the 19th century. Behavioral psychology research has given way to cognitive approaches, and subsequently to situated or connectionist views, but the empirical findings have consistently advanced. Our understanding of learning, though not yet complete, still provides a robust basis for designing instruction—or, more properly, creating experiences that facilitate learning.

The scientific methods that are used for studying learning vary—qualitative studies detailing the thoughts of individual learners sit alongside quantitative studies that use objective instruments, and at times we use both as converging evidence. We also coordinate with theory. And we reject studies that don't provide enough detail or present details that violate known standards for quality.

In general, scientific studies will say:

- Here's what I believe to be true (and why it's important).
- Here's a way to tell if it's true, and what would say it's true.
- Here's what I found when I did that.
- This is what we can now say about what I believed.
- Here's what's next.

Science isn't total knowledge and final wisdom, however. Scientists can disagree, and this is beneficial to the field. There are also those who falsify data (although typically we eventually uncover those deceptions). As scientists work to resolve our disagreements, we advance our understanding. We conduct experiments that address our knowledge gaps, and we replicate studies that violate our expectations. We may have hiccups, but we continue increasing our understanding over time.

An additional barrier to having a complete base of knowledge is finding the science we need to back up our design choices. There aren't always specific studies that address the issues we're interested in; or, if they do exist, they may be difficult to find. (Because many studies exist behind a paywall, you can't access them without the considerable expenditures that only university libraries can muster.)

When experimental data aren't a sufficient base for design, the next best step is to go to a theory that's relevant. If you can't find a study on whether group discussion is more effective for ambiguous domains than individual challenges, look to theory. Here, social learning theory might suggest that discussing ambiguities would be more powerful than trying to train an individual on all the shades of grey. In short, frameworks and theories, based upon sound frameworks, provide a sound basis of inference for design when science is inadequate.

However, more often than not, you'll discover robust findings that provide guidance.

This Is Your Brain on Learning

To truly be able to comprehend the arguments and develop talent, you need to understand a wee bit about the cognitive science of learning. This background will support you in interpreting the refutations to follow. It will also help you determine good learning design, and understand new advances.

As an initial premise, our learning goals are twofold: *retention over time until needed* and *transfer to all appropriate situations*. We want to use cues in the environment to activate patterns of neurons that represent the appropriate actions. When we can react in context appropriately, we can say we've learned what we need to. This transfer might be narrow, say to a specific device or instance, in which case we frequently refer to training. Sometimes this retrieval is broad, perhaps applying specific skills like negotiation in many different contexts, and we're more likely to term that education. Regardless, we want people to retrieve the necessary abilities when required.

When we activate patterns of neurons in conjunction with one another, their relationships get stronger ("neurons that fire together, wire together"). And that's about all that's really relevant at the neural level (see NeuroX or BrainX). Most of what happens is better addressed at the cognitive level. The important implication is that you need to activate the relevant neurons. In fact, pre-activating the neurons helps with the strengthening. This means that activating relevant knowledge is a valuable precursor to a learning experience. For instance, during a training, you can mention previous lessons or draw attention to known problems that require a new skill to address.

However, there's only so much strengthening that can happen at any one time, because the system will fatigue. To put it simply, you quite literally need sleep before you can learn more. The implication is that to strengthen what you've learned to the point it's persistent, you will likely need to deactivate (rest or sleep) and reactivate it multiple times. Thus, we need to *space* learning over time, allowing us to retrieve the learning and activate the specific elements using cues in the environment. We activate it to develop the links, and then reactivate it by finding cues that retrieve the necessary neural patterns. We associate various environmental situations as appropriate for this pattern to activate.

To make sure that what we learn can be flexibly activated in different conditions, it helps to mix in activation for one thing with another—mixing retrieval practices. We might bring in another skill in between or vary contexts. This strengthens the links in the face of conflicting signals. It has also been shown that retrieving in context is superior to abstract retrieval. To generate the ability to transfer broadly requires exposure to more disparate contexts—ideally contexts that span the space of appropriate practice. As a result, we abstract across the different contexts, creating a transcendent representation that we can re-instantiate in the new context.

To guide our behavior, we create explanations of how the world works, and use that to develop our ability to respond. So, for example, we might use an analogy of water flowing through pipes to diagnose an electronic circuit. These mental models, built upon causal relationships, are the basis for making better decisions. (And I'll maintain that making better decisions is likely to be the most valuable lesson for organizations going forward.) An interesting result is that learners will build models because it's an inherent feature of our cognitive architecture. But if it's not a good model, learners won't replace it, they'll simply try to patch it. Consequently, it's best to provide a good model up front that.explains what to do.

Using examples, we can help learners understand how the model is applied to solve real problems. Here we establish a context with an undesirable state, and demonstrate how the model drives the process to a solution. Showing the underlying thinking behind the steps and portraying the example in the form of a story are both demonstrably valuable. It has also been shown that representing mistakes in the process of problem solving, and documenting the back-tracking and repair, helps learners internalize the self-monitoring principles. It can be hard to find experts who are willing to admit mistakes, but it's valuable for the learning outcome. The contexts seen in examples and practice guide the transfer of learning to appropriate situations.

Ultimately, learning is a probabilistic game. To paraphrase Dorothy Parker: "You can lead a learner to learning, but you can't make them think." What we do, as designers, is create environments that increase or optimize the likelihood that the necessary learning will occur. Using what's known in learning science is an important component to getting this right. Myths, superstitions, and misconceptions undermine our effectiveness.

Limitations and Conflicts

As mentioned, even within science there are disagreements. Some things others have called myths, I have found a useful interpretation for. Similarly, things others have cited, I will argue against. This is the nature of science— some ideas and theories are debatable (see 70-20-10 and Problem-Based Learning). In this book, I separate out myths from misconceptions; I'll explain my interpretation for the misconceptions, in addition to what the science says, with the focus on finding value.

I've also separated out a whole section on beliefs about learning design that are detrimental to the industry. They don't all have specific studies to refute them, so some of the arguments are drawn from general cognitive and learning science theories. Still, the reasons outlined are sound enough to reject these beliefs. This doesn't mean that you can just wing it—"Science doesn't agree, so I can do what I want," is not the appropriate response.

And finally, very quickly, I want to shed light on my experience with the science of learning and other learning research—and the challenges of scholarly publishing. I served on the editorial board of *The British Journal of Educational Technology* (*BJET*) and review submissions for other journals (including *Instructional Science*). I've also been on the program committees for a number of scientific conferences in learning and technology. I tell you this to let you know that I've reviewed *a lot* of draft articles, and I can state that many fail even the most basic tests. (A study on reviewers for *BJET* documented that I rejected around two-thirds of the ones I saw, not including asking for major revisions. And that's still slightly more generous than the journal's editor!) The pressure to publish is tremendous, and the resources for most academics are few, so it's important to recognize the characteristics of quality research, and the flaws that can limit the implications of the work. Thus, not every published study has utility for workplace learning, and some may even have flaws that constrain what can be inferred.

LEARNING MYTHS

Myth has several definitions. A common interpretation holds that myths are stories that explain our origin and our place in the universe. However, that's not what I am talking about in this book. I'm referring to beliefs we hold that aren't true. These beliefs can be stated as scientific fact or be based on inferences from observation. They can also have an appeal that makes them plausible. And, unfortunately, persistent.

The Brain and Learning Project of the UK's Organisation for Economic Co-operation and Development (OECD) talked specifically about neuromyths (many of which are listed here), and defined them as "a misconception generated by a misunderstanding, a misreading, or a misquoting of facts scientifically established (by brain research) to make a case for the use of brain research in education or other contexts" (OECD 2002). The origin of these myths isn't always discernable, but it's likely to be a combination of intuitive appeal, the appearance of support from dubious or misinterpreted science, and a lack of desire and ability to penetrate the academese of the original research. These are the myths that affect the learning industry. These beliefs are robust in marketing and writing, and are acted upon as a matter of design and implementation. You hear calls to design to accommodate these beliefs, or use tools that are specifically supposed to address the issues.

The obvious problem? *They're not true.* To the extent we accommodate these myths we are, in practice, wasting valuable resources. If you make purchasing decisions or invest resources based on these myths, you're being misled.

Our field should have a level of professionalism—we should not be committing "learning malpractice." To that end, let's take a look at these learning myths. While there's no claim that the list is exhaustive, and research may eventually emerge to support one or another, at this point none of these myths pass the sniff test of conscious (and informed) reflection, nor do they stand up to scientific scrutiny.

"My learning
style is to cheat."

LEARNING STYLES:
ADAPTATION

THE CLAIM

We should adapt learning to learners based
on their learning styles.

The belief in learning styles has persisted across education and organizational learning for decades, dating back as far as the 1970s with the Dunn and Dunn Learning Style Model. The most important manifestation of this is that if we can identify a learner's style, we should adapt our training to their learning style for the best impact.

Let's be clear about what I mean by *learning style*. A learning style is an identifiable proclivity, either favoring or performing better with a specific way in which learning can differ. This has often meant differentiating between visual, auditory, or kinesthetic modalities (seeing, hearing, or acting). Another proposed difference would be whether to present abstract ideas before concrete examples or vice versa. Or, if the learner learns better alone or with others. The list goes on.

The question behind this claim is: If we can reliably identify these differences, should we take them into account?

Adapting the training to the learner might mean one of two things:

- We cater to the learner's learning style by providing them with materials that facilitate their learning.
- We challenge them to ensure their learning is persistent in the face of adversity and to develop their abilities in areas that have room for growth.

THE APPEAL

It's clear that learners differ. What's more, we know that different approaches work well for different learners. Identifying those differences and leveraging them for the learner's, or the training's, benefit would be a useful use of that knowledge.

THE POTENTIAL UPSIDE

If, in fact, we *can* identify a learner's strengths, it gives us options to improve the learning process. For one, we could shorten their learning time by playing to their strengths. Alternatively, we could develop them to be stronger performers by challenging them against their weaknesses.

THE POTENTIAL DOWNSIDE

If this doesn't actually have any benefit, investing in adapting training to a learner's style would result in wasted resources because you've unnecessarily developed the redundancy necessary to support different strokes for different folks.

HOW TO EVALUATE

To test the hypothesis that learners have distinct styles in which they learn best, a certain type of data are necessary—data that demonstrate a reliable difference in outcomes using different treatments on different populations.

In 2008, psychology professor Harold Pashler of the University of California, San Diego, and colleagues, under a commission from the Psychological Science in the Public Interest initiative, searched for such studies on learning styles. They took the ones they found and eliminated those that didn't provide a sufficient basis for normalization (such as enough quantitative rigor to allow them to be compared). One criteria they used to find these studies was that they had to show that "the learning method that optimizes test performance of one learning-style group is different from the learning method that optimizes the test performance of a second learning-style group." Technically, it's called a *crossover interaction*. They then examined the remaining set.

WHAT THE EVIDENCE SAYS

Pashler and colleagues found *no* convincing data that met their criteria. They found one study with questionable outcomes supporting the hypothesis (Sternberg et al. 1999), as well as several studies with solid design that demonstrated no benefit.

They concluded "that at present, there is no adequate evidence base to justify incorporating learning-styles assessments into general educational practice" (Pashler et al. 2008). In short, the evidence was inadequate. While people can express preferences, attempts to adapt learning to learning styles appear to have no significant impact.

That's not to say that there won't eventually be an effective learning style instrument and an associated solution that will work. For example, it's possible that while learners are developing initial capability, it might serve to play to whatever style is ultimately identified, and then later as they develop capability it makes sense to challenge them. At this point, however, it doesn't make sense to adapt course material *on the basis of learning styles.*

WHAT TO DO

If you want to adapt learning design to different styles (and there are sound reasons to do so), there are sound bases upon which to do so. The best basis is upon the learner's performance: Are they struggling with the practice? If so, simplify the problems they are working on until they've demonstrated mastery. If they're doing well, increase the challenge. You can also choose problems closer in context to and farther from their particular situation.

CITATIONS

Pashler, H., M. McDaniel, D. Rohrer, and R. Bjork. 2008. "Learning Styles: Concepts and Evidence." *Psychological Science in the Public Interest* 9(3): 105-119.

Sternberg, R.J., E.L. Grigorenko, M. Ferrari, and P. Clinkenbeard. 1999. "A Triarchic Analysis of an Aptitude–Treatment Interaction." *European Journal of Psychological Assessment* 15:1-11.

LEARNING STYLES: MEASUREMENT

THE CLAIM

We can reliably categorize individuals by their learning styles.

The persistent belief in learning styles has been touted continuously for decades. The claim is that learning styles are distinct and persistent, and they can be measured. This entails having clear discriminations between how people learn, and the ability to systematically assign individuals to a particular characterization.

We've created a wide variety of instruments to differentiate people. Not all are identified as learning styles, so personality types, leadership styles, and sensory format preferences are among the ways in which people have been sorted. And there are also a wide variety of dimensions proposed, ranging from your sense modality (auditory, visual, and so forth), level of social skill, ability to work abstractly or concretely, holistic or detail, and so on.

Empirically, these categorizations *are* being used for a wide variety of purposes: to alter learning, to choose for various roles, even to make hiring (and firing) decisions. So the obvious question is whether we can reliably identify learning styles.

THE APPEAL

Intuitively, we know people differ as learners. Anyone who has worked with learners recognizes that they differ in substantive ways. Elements that influence learning and contribute to learner success include cognitive factors such as ability to do deductive and inductive learning, affective factors such as extroversion and compliance, and cognative factors such as motivation and anxiety.

The appeal, then, is that if we can ascertain how any learner learns, we can use that to their advantage. On this basis, if we can identify individuals according to their learning approach, we can make adaptations that make learning more effective.

THE POTENTIAL UPSIDE

If we can reliably identify how people learn, we can do one of two things:

- Tailor learning for them.
- Challenge them and develop their other ways to learn.

A positive use is to help individuals see that while others differ, these differences are valuable. Research does show that diversity helps, so if people can reliably be categorized, ensuring that different characteristics are present at appropriate times would be a valuable addition.

THE POTENTIAL DOWNSIDE

If we're wrong, measuring individuals and assigning labels may limit them. Similarly, we might misuse these instruments under the belief that they're legitimate, causing us to make hiring or work assignment decisions based upon an invalid basis.

Moreover, we could be investing money in differentiated training that isn't really viable. We would be wasting money.

HOW TO EVALUATE

Categorizing people falls under the science of psychometrics, literally "measuring the mind." As background, valid categorizations need to meet at least four tests to determine they are valid:

- **internal consistency:** the different dimensions are truly independent from each other
- **test-retest reliability:** individuals reliably measure the same on repeated applications
- **construct validity:** the questions measure what they claim to measure
- **predictive validity:** the assessed dimensions have a consistent and useful impact.

It is important to note that you want *independent* research. Any research conducted by the owner of a proprietary instrument is suspect. Unless the research has been published in a peer-reviewed journal with sufficient overview of the theoretic formulation and methodology to support scrutiny and replication, such data don't provide sufficient scientific credibility. Thus, to evaluate the instruments, independent published research in all four areas is required.

WHAT THE EVIDENCE SAYS

In 2004, a panel of scientists led by Frank Coffield was assembled to evaluate learning styles. They identified 71 instruments, and chose a representative sample of 13 influential models to evaluate. These models were typically the best-known or most widely used instruments (including familiar names such as Myers–Briggs and Kolb). They compiled and assessed independent research that evaluated the instruments on these characteristics.

Only one instrument, of one dimension, met all four criteria. Several others were rated of interest (but these are, with one exception, essentially unknown in the market). Furthermore, none were considered appropriate for organizational learning. The instruments by Vermunt and Entwistle (both are open research exercises) held the most promise as potential learning style instruments. However, there were no meaningful instruments that met the basics.

The area of personality psychology is looking at reliable categorizations, and their work is converging on the OCEAN model (openness, conscientiousness, extroversion, agreeableness, and neuroticism). They have established psychometric validity, but as of 2017 it hadn't been operationalized for learning. And perhaps shouldn't be.

Note also that almost all the instruments use self-report, asking individuals to internally reflect and make subjective judgments about themselves. This is, in general, fraught with peril. Our beliefs about our own behavior are notoriously inaccurate. Some instruments use better questions that ask about our behavior, rather than our own reflections, but it's still possible to infer and game the questions. Ideally, such evaluations would be based upon our actual behaviors, whether observed in situ or in simulations. So, this is an area of concern.

WHAT TO DO

The biggest recommendation is to design for the material, not the learner. That is, use the learning science recommendations for how to teach what you're trying to teach. In addition, you can provide support for the potential barriers that different learners might face, such as comprehending complex models.

It should be noted that a wide variety of instruments were not included in the study, and even those that were included and identified as flawed are still being used. Moreover, more appear all the time. The big issue is the validity of the instruments. As Coffield and colleagues commented, the proprietary nature of the instruments restricts the free exchange of research to establish replicability, and thus draws into question the actual validity of the research.

Note that, one day, we could and should be able to reliably identify learners on some dimensions. The problem right now is based on the theoretical grounds of creating a sound basis for differentiating, and then creating suitable instruments to assess those dimensions. Again, it's not to say that learners don't differ, but instead to say that as yet, we can't reliably identify how, where, and when.

CITATION

Coffield, F., D. Mosely, E. Hall, and K. Ecclestone. 2004. *Should We Be Using Learning Styles? What Research Has to Say to Practice.* London: Learning & Skills Research Centre.

"Good thing the program is only 9 seconds long!"

ATTENTION SPAN OF A GOLDFISH

THE CLAIM

Humans have changed to having the attention span of a goldfish.

With the advent of mobile devices, we're now working on smaller screens, in more contexts, but also with greater interruptions. There's an argument that technology is changing the way we think—jumping between different tasks as something new and flashy grabs our attention. Thus, the possibility is that we're developing shorter attention spans.

The model most touted is that our attention span is now less than that of a goldfish; they can manage nine seconds while we can sustain our interest for only eight. This suggests that we need to cut our content down to an incredible extent. If we don't, we risk losing people.

THE APPEAL

There certainly are an increasing number of devices, and people are looking at them for shorter amounts of time in many instances. Youth, in particular, seem to spend less time on one thing than another. It caters to some observations we make, and sounds like a guilty pleasure observation about human nature.

THE POTENTIAL UPSIDE

If this is true, we must shorten our content into chunks that learners can more easily digest. Having the awareness, at least, means we can address it in the processes we use, rather than being victim to this outcome. We can cut down our messages, provide more variety, and use more attention-getting approaches.

THE POTENTIAL DOWNSIDE

If this isn't true, we could be deluding ourselves *about* ourselves, and not giving ourselves credit where credit is due. We might miss the opportunity to leverage sustained engagement to accomplish our goals.

HOW TO EVALUATE

There are two paths to look at here. For one, we can look at research on attention, and the physiological bases. What do we know about attention? What is the likelihood it is malleable within our lifespans?

We can also look for counter-examples. If we can find examples of people persisting in attention beyond the purported barrier, we can suggest that there's a weak basis to believe that attention spans are shortening.

Of course, first, we should determine whether the original claim is legitimate or not. Was there a plausible trail of research?

WHAT THE EVIDENCE SAYS

The original data for this claim were cited from research by Microsoft Canada. Patti Shank, among others, discovered that the claim came from an infographic in a report (from Microsoft Canada Advertising), which was sourced from a separate site called Statistic Brain, which cited another study on browser use (phew!). The eight-second figure came from average time on pages in that study, which is a very limited sense of attention. (Worse, there's no citation for the attention span of a goldfish that humans were compared to.) This is a sensationalist bit of misleading data in a rather more complicated story.

Attention is too complex to be lumped under a number such as eight seconds. Research on attention, such as that done by Sharlene Newman, Tim Keller, and Marcel Just of Carnegie Mellon University in 2007, has shown that it is largely under volitional control; we decide what we want to attend to! That is, we can choose what to focus on, and what to tune out.

Of course, this isn't the complete story, as there are certain circumstances under which our attention can be captured despite our intentions. When we hear certain salient words, such as our names or a word with some likely entailments of notoriety (like sex), our attention can be stolen. This is the famous "cocktail party phenomenon." Similarly, movement in the periphery of our vision can draw our visual attention away from the area of desired focus (remember how hard it is to read text on a website if there are flashing GIFs in the margins?).

Similarly, there are many examples of extended attention. Two prominent ones are movies and video games. Individuals can engage in a movie for several hours, and the problems with video-game addiction would certainly run counter to an argument of limited attention.

Changing our attention spans on a physiological basis would require evolution to take its long course. Instead, what we're seeing is simply an increased number of distractions that make it easier to consider shifting our attention. And with more distractors, we may be more finicky about how long we're willing to devote our attention.

However, fundamentally, we're still capable of dedicating the same level of attention we've been able to demonstrate for generations. The evolutionary status hasn't changed.

WHAT TO DO

Despite the lack of necessity for constraining our content, there are reasons why we *should* still look to minimize content. It's too easy to throw everything into the learning bucket instead of winnowing down the quantity to the minimum amount necessary to succeed.

Similarly, finding intrinsic interest to help sustain a desire to pay attention is also a good design principle. Just because we *can* pay attention doesn't mean we *will*, unless there's a compelling reason. Leveraging that is in alignment with our attentional system.

CITATIONS

Newman, S.D., T.A. Keller, and M.A. Just. 2007. "Volitional Control of Attention and Brain Activation in Dual Task Performance." *Human Brain Mapping* 28(2): 109-117.

Shank, P. 2017. *Attention and the 8-Second Span.* eLearning Industry, April 4. https://elearningindustry.com/8-second-attention-span-organizational-learning.

"But Mom, I can get my homework done while watching a movie! We kids can multitask!"

MULTITASKING

THE CLAIM

We can effectively multitask across a number of attention-requiring actions.

The multitasking myth relates to the "attention span of a goldfish" myth mentioned previously; it suggests that we can manage more things at once. The argument comes from the increased practice of toggling between multiple windows on desktop computers or jumping between different apps and notifications on mobile devices.

The claim is that we can do this effectively. That is (and if not for all folks, certainly for young folks), we can successfully manage multiple tasks at the same time, with no decrease in performance.

THE APPEAL

Those who could successfully do this would certainly have an advantage on others. If we can successfully multitask—or learn to multitask—we can appeal to our desire for continuing stimulation with no decrement in the outcomes. We are more powerful than we would be if not. After all, time is a fixed resource, so the appeal lies in performing multiple tasks at once to cram more into your day or finish them more quickly. And we certainly see examples—my favorite being a mother keeping house and cooking dinner, all while monitoring her kids.

THE POTENTIAL UPSIDE

If this is true, it means that we can be *more* effective in our work. We can handle more tasks at once, making us better workers and potentially more successful. We'd like to believe that the increasing pressures of day-to-day life aren't diminishing the quality of our work.

THE POTENTIAL DOWNSIDE

If this isn't true, of course, we run the risk of decreased performance. Those who are multitasking are wasting time and deluding themselves. If we persist in this belief, things will take longer and/or have less quality.

HOW TO EVALUATE

To understand whether multitasking makes sense, we need to understand the mental operations behind it. And to do this, we need to understand our cognitive architecture. It turns out that our conscious processing is serial in nature;

that is, we can do only one thing at a time. The underlying processing is parallel, but we think in linear forms.

Now, multitasking is for conscious effort. Automated (read: well-practiced) behaviors can operate independently on our parallel systems, but any explicit thinking—problem solving, design, and so on—is inherently conscious. This means that it's running on our linear system.

To evaluate this claim, we need to survey a wide variety of research on task switching, and look at the evidence. Does a deterioration in performance when task switching go beyond the switch, and involve some sort of additional overhead on the change—a switching "cost"?

WHAT THE EVIDENCE SAYS

To multitask, we have to switch conscious attention between tasks. And while our brains don't quite work like computers, we can use the analogical reasoning here. To switch between tasks, we have to stop the current task, save the current state, retrieve the other state, regenerate our status, and then process on it until we switch again. And this extra saving and retrieval overhead slows us down.

In fact, research suggests that there are switching costs. The models differ, but the empirical results hold: Switching deteriorates performance beyond just the change. Doing the heavy lifting, the American Psychological Association (2006) summarized the multitasking research: "Although switch costs may be relatively small, . . . they can add up to large amounts." The APA concluded that multitasking cuts efficiency and raises risks.

Take, for example, driving. Those of us who drive, after a certain learning period, are pretty accomplished at it. In fact, we can drive home on a familiar route while holding a conversation, solving a problem, whatever. It's so well-practiced that even if we *intend* to stop on the way home or detour, we can end up at home and have forgotten our stop or side-trip if we start thinking about an issue or talking to someone during the drive.

Here's the catch, however. If we suddenly have a traffic snarl, our attention has to go to driving and we'll stop the conversation or the thinking. This is why a conversation with someone in the car is less problematic than a conversation with someone on the phone: the person in the car will also notice the problem and cease talking, and maybe even help!

The phenomenon of switching between tasks seems fast enough that it can feel continuous. So if we're playing a familiar computer game, listening to music, and talking to our friend, it may appear that we're doing it all at once, but we're really switching between tasks. It's just that when conversing, playing a game that's been automated, and listening to a familiar song, most of our attention is on the content of the conversation. Note what happens, however, if a new song comes on or the game suddenly gets complex.

WHAT TO DO

The quick answer is to reduce the need to multitask. Design systems that minimize cognitive load, so actions map to tasks and interfaces integrate the necessary information.

Then, when designing learning, simplify problems initially and gradually introduce complexity. If learners must perform in a complex environment, gradually automate what can be automated so they're keeping their conscious attention free for those things that vary and require active problem solving.

CITATION

American Psychological Association. 2006. "Multi-tasking: Switching Costs." www.apa.org/research/action/multitask.aspx.

"So if I *do it* and *hear it*, I'll remember it 100%!"

DALE'S CONE

THE CLAIM

People remember 10 percent of what they read and 90 percent of what they do.

The claim here, attributed to educator Edgar Dale and popularized in numerous images presenting a striated, or layered, cone, is that people remember:
- 10 percent of what they read
- 20 percent of what they hear
- 30 percent of what they see
- 50 percent of what they see and hear
- 70 percent of what they say and write
- 90 percent of what they do.

This has been massaged in a number of ways, with specifics for teaching. So, you can variously find 90 percent is real practice (where 70 percent is a presentation), or 70 percent is to practice and 90 percent is to teach others.

THE APPEAL

The appeal is that Dale's Cone provides a sound basis for going beyond presentation. It suggests that we need to *do* to learn. It also gives a basis to consider augmenting practice with other forms of activity.

THE POTENTIAL UPSIDE

If this model of the learning effects of various approaches is valid, it provides a strong argument for designing learning that involves practice. Having a definitive guide to media effectiveness is a valuable adjunct to what we do.

THE POTENTIAL DOWNSIDE

If the provenance of the data is questionable, it undermines having an easy solution to determine the learning approach. It might mean we have to work harder to determine the appropriate media to use for particular tasks.

HOW TO EVALUATE

You can evaluate this claim in two ways:
- Examine the original source of the data and determine its veracity.
- Assess the validity of the numbers at face value.

In both cases, Will Thalheimer has done this research, first alone, and then in conjunction with some academics and published their conclusions.

WHAT THE EVIDENCE SAYS

The original diagram, from Edgar Dale's 1946 book *Audio-Visual Methods in Teaching*, was presented without numbers (and with an admonition to not take it too seriously). Numbers were subsequently added, with no clear indication of by who or when. In another case, a diagram purporting to show such numbers was attributed to researcher Micki Chi and associates. Will Thalheimer and colleagues found the representations to be fallacious, with no data to support them (Subramony et al. 2014).

Essentially, the original cone was repeatedly and successively misappropriated, including adding numbers and more to support a particular need. In addition, the false data attributed to Chi and others are, frankly, learning malfeasance. The people doing so either didn't have sufficient diligence (the most positive interpretation), or were deliberately promoting it for some unknown purpose.

Further, the numbers should be suspect even without any of the other considerations. Seldom does research reveal such perfectly round numbers. Rounding might make sense if they were close, but it's just too bracketed to be useful.

WHAT TO DO

It's true that practice is a necessary part of learning, but it's not just "do it and you'll retain 90 percent of what you learn." You have to determine the sufficient amount of practice to yield 90 percent retention (if that's your goal). Better yet, provide practice and assess until learners achieve the level of performance you need (at the time they need it).

Similarly, you should determine the role of supporting media. There are roles for reading, visuals, and audition, but they are specific to the task and the learning need.

CITATIONS

Dale, E. 1946. *Audio-Visual Methods in Teaching.* New York: Dryden Press.

Subramony, D., M. Molenda, A. Betrus, and W. Thalheimer. 2014. "The Mythical Retention Chart and the Corruption of Dale's Cone of Experience." *Educational Technology* 54(6): 6-16.

GENERATIONS

THE CLAIM

Individual workplace values can be characterized by the era in which people were born.

In the past few years, there's been quite a bit of concern about the newest generation to the workforce, the Millennials. These new arrivals come from college after having grown up in the late 1990s and early 2000s. As a result, they are compared to the other workforce generations.

The three generations most prominently in the workforce today are roughly characterized as having been born in the ranges of 1946-1964 (Baby Boomers), 1965-1984 (Generation X), and 1982-2004 (Millennials). Note that there is some discrepancy about the characterizations of the age ranges, but these have the benefit of having roughly similar durations. I'm ignoring, by the way, the traditionalists, born 1945 or before, as they're largely already out of the workforce, and the post-Millennials (still to be named) born after 2004, who haven't yet joined the workforce in considerable numbers.

The main component of the claim is that these generational groups differ on various characteristics—for example, what they value, how they work, and even how they learn. This has to do with what the world was like when they grew up. The Boomers grew up with parents back from the war and a relatively safe world. Television had innocuous shows that demonstrated family values and heroism. Generation X grew up with the "me" decade; more of them went to college, but they were also latchkey kids, left alone more after school as their parents worked. Millennials are considered to be more likely to see divorce, and have been more sheltered. These different experiences as a generation are the basis for the claim for substantive differences in how these generations act.

THE APPEAL

The appeal has to do with the obvious differences between younger and older people. Everything from "kids these days" to "not your father's Oldsmobile" all have roots in some obvious differences. And there certainly have been changes in popular media through the years—for example, more anti-hero roles in movies—which reflect changing preferences. For learning, there have been proposals about how we need to adapt learning to these new learners, in terms of attention, multitasking, and devices. If indeed the generations differ, this would make sense.

THE POTENTIAL UPSIDE

If generations differ in how they work and learn, there are important implications. If we can identify those differences, we can adapt accordingly. We can manage differently and design our learning to be best suited for each generation. We would not want the same learning experience for Millennials as we would for Generation X, let alone Baby Boomers. This ensures that we're adapting to people effectively.

THE POTENTIAL DOWNSIDE

If there aren't substantial differences based upon when people were born, we could be making investments and adaptations that aren't justifiable. In fact, doing so could serve as a form of discrimination, in that we're treating people differently based on an arbitrary factor out of their control: their birth date.

HOW TO EVALUATE

We can address this claim in several ways. One is to survey a wide selection of people to see whether their birth date affects what they value in the workplace. Do they want different things based on their generation? We can also try to segregate differences by age or experience. That is, can we explain the differences by the age of the individuals, rather than their generation?

WHAT THE EVIDENCE SAYS

When they surveyed individuals, Jennifer Mencl and Scott W. Lester found no significant differences in what people wanted by their generation. That is, the values people placed on various aspects of workplace relationships weren't tied to their generation. And data on similarities versus differences from another study by Scott W. Lester and colleagues showed that while each generation perceives itself as being more different from other generations, that perception did not reflect how much they actually differed. People's perceptions often don't match reality, and that appears to be the case here.

In either guise, generations or just Millennials, most differences aren't significant and the differences that exist are easier to explain by age than by the circumstances experienced during their formative years. It's also fair to imagine that the differences between individuals have a greater impact than the differences between the popular media of their youth. If you grew up in a broken home, in any generation, you will have a different perspective than someone who didn't, and you'll have more in common with those who did than those who watched similar television shows and movies. And those different eras don't obviously have direct correlation to the purported generations.

Further, the differences that are seen, such as a greater interest in certification among the young, have a plausible alternative hypothesis. If you don't have lots of experience to point to—no "been there, done that"—you'd like to at least point to a course you've had on the topic, regardless of your age *or* generation.

WHAT TO DO

The short response is not to segregate based on age: We should be addressing individuals by their demonstrated behaviors and competencies, not their birth date.

CITATIONS

Lester, S.W., R.L. Standifer, N.J. Schultz, and J.M. Windsor. 2012. "Actual Versus Perceived Generational Differences at Work: An Empirical Examination." *Journal of Leadership & Organizational Studies* 19:341-354.

Mencl, J., and S.W. Lester. 2014. "More Alike Than Different: What Generations Value and How the Values Affect Employee Workplace Perceptions." *Journal of Leadership & Organizational Studies* 21(3): 257-272.

"I'm going native!"

DIGITAL NATIVES

THE CLAIM

Those who grew up in the digital age
have unique skills with technology.

There's a belief that young people, those who grew up with digital technology, have a natural facility with this technology that others, specifically older people, simply can't emulate. They've been surrounded by this technology their whole lives, so in some sense using technology in the workplace is as natural to them as breathing (like to a fish, water is invisible). This was an idea propagated not least by Marc Prensky in his 2001 book *Digital Natives, Digital Immigrants*.

A milder claim might be that younger people have no fear of technology, even if they do not necessarily possess natural skills *with* the technology.

THE APPEAL

Psychologist L.S. Vygotsky and media theorist Marshall McLuhan, among many others, argue that the technology you use fundamentally changes the way you think. Thus, kids who've grown up with technology know no other life, and see electronic devices and tools as simply part of their environment. Moreover, they have developed skills with these technologies that others who weren't immersed in technology simply *can't* acquire.

THE POTENTIAL UPSIDE

If such innate skills are indeed the case, we could do a couple of practical things. For one, if we could assume digital skills on the part of young people, we wouldn't need to introduce them to new ways of doing things if they're technologically mediated. And we could partner older people with young people for support; otherwise, we may need to continue supporting older folks with technology scaffolding.

THE POTENTIAL DOWNSIDE

If this natural ability isn't the case, we could make the mistake of not adequately supporting young people in using technology effectively. We might make assumptions about the distributions of skills that are inappropriate.

HOW TO EVALUATE

A comprehensive evaluation of people's familiarity with technology would survey the existing literature to see what's said. Such studies should identify the factors that characterize differences in ability with the Internet. Age or generation could be one, but so could other factors. If the factors aren't age, then we can't argue for an inherent benefit to the young.

WHAT THE EVIDENCE SAYS

Researchers Christopher Jones and Binhui Shao conducted a literature review on this topic in 2011. While focused on implications for higher education, their results carry over into the workplace (not least because students at that time now are in the workplace). While the initial studies they reviewed showed differences in familiarity, more nuanced studies found that there weren't specific differences in their ability to use the technology well.

What the studies on digital nativism found was that young folks were no better at leveraging technology effectively than older folks. Any cultural immersion or lack of fear of technology didn't manifest as preternatural skills. They were not more eager adopters nor more facile in use. The conclusion of Jones and Shao (2011) was "there is no evidence that there is a single new generation of young students entering Higher Education and the terms Net Generation and Digital Native do not capture the processes of change that are taking place."

WHAT TO DO

It is a mistake to assume that young people are effective technology users—and that older people are automatically less effective. Young people might be comfortable using it, but their skills should be assessed and addressed just like everyone else. The first thing to do is not to determine individual skills by age or any other categorical means to address, but instead to identify specific skills.

Note also that a lack of facility may not be the same as a lack of fear. There are reasons to believe that young folks may be comfortable with technology, but someone else's lack of comfort could mask an actual ability.

CITATION

Jones, C., and B. Shao. 2011. "The Net Generation and Digital Natives: Implications for Higher Education." New York: Higher Education Academy.

"Consuming content is the new way to learn!"

DIGITAL MEANS WE LEARN DIFFERENTLY

THE CLAIM

Human learning is about to change forever.

I took this claim from a recent whitepaper promoted by a major industry magazine. There were a number of claims embodied, covering everything from virtual and augmented realities to neural implants. The underlying theme was that with technology, our brains will learn in new and fundamental ways.

This view is repeated in claims that as our kids learn with and through technology, they're learning differently from previous generations who did not grow up the same way. Presumably, we learned differently when we shifted from apprenticeships to the classroom, and this is a similar shift. There's no doubt we are learning through new means.

THE APPEAL

The associated premise for this claim, as promoted by researchers like L.S. Vygotsky and Marshall McLuhan, is that the technology we use is fundamentally changing the way we think and perform. For example, we resort to Google to look up information instead of remembering it. (In fact, there's an argument that search is making us stupider.) Since our behaviors are clearly changing, this means that there's something new and important going on.

THE POTENTIAL UPSIDE

If we are learning in new ways, the implicit associated idea is that we'll be able to bypass the slow process of neural strengthening. The extreme view is that we'll effectively be able to download new knowledge into our brains. The opportunity to learn in new ways, not just more efficiently, is very appealing. We might be able to do away with schools!

THE POTENTIAL DOWNSIDE

If we really aren't learning in new ways, we could be spending a lot of effort in ways that don't align with our brains. We might step away from what's known about effective learning, and move into some dream realm. For instance, we might let artificial intelligence systems parse content and create questions, and think that answering those knowledge questions will lead to valuable new skills.

HOW TO EVALUATE

Learning is a neural change at its core. So, if we're learning differently, our cognitive architecture has to change. Is there evidence that our brains are changing as a result of using technology?

There's no real way to counter this with a study. How do you "prove" that we aren't learning differently? This is really a theoretical argument, and we have to go to causal mechanisms to understand why it doesn't make sense.

WHAT THE EVIDENCE SAYS

Changes in our neural architecture are accomplished by two methods: learning and evolution, as theorists Robert N. Brandon and Norbert Hornstein laid out. Evolution is a very slow process, occurring over thousands of years or more. This is genotypic plasticity; we change the genes. Given that the digital revolution is only in the tens of years, our genes are unlikely to have changed. Learning itself, which changes the brain wiring, is a process of action and reflection. It's phenotypic plasticity; we may not change the animal, but we can create learning that changes their capability. And while we might change the conditions under which action occurs (simulation instead of apprenticeship, for instance), it's using the same mechanisms of neural strengthening. Thus, there's no way that digital is fundamentally changing the way we learn.

If you want to argue that we are changing the mechanisms by which we support learning, I'd agree that we can be doing much better: virtual reality can enhance the immersive nature of learning, and context-sensitive mechanisms can be more effective at detecting "teachable moments" and extending learning beyond the classroom. And this is good (when done well). But it's not changing learning, it's changing instruction.

Thus, what technology could be changing is what we learn. That is, we could be learning how to use technology to improve things we used to do in old ways, and even new things we can do. This doesn't change how we learn, but what we learn with and what we learn about.

WHAT TO DO

We do want to use technology in ways that align with how our brains work: challenging us to take actions and providing feedback. Using technology to do that better is great and should be lauded. Still, stick to the basics of human learning: Practice and feedback lead to retention and transfer. There is no shortcut. We can be more effective and more efficient, but we're not seeing a fundamental shift in how we learn because of new digital technologies.

CITATION

Brandon, R.N., and N. Hornstein. 1986. "From Icons to Symbols: Some Speculations on the Origins of Language." *Biology and Philosophy* 1:169-189.

"Here, you handle this, it's not in my wheelhouse."

LEFT AND RIGHT BRAIN

THE CLAIM

People can be characterized by their relative proportion of left- and right-brain capabilities.

The areas of higher functions in the brain are divided into two hemispheres, and research has suggested that there are different functions in each half of the brain. The general suggestion is that the left brain is for systematic work like mathematics and logic, whereas the right brain is more integrative and creative. This probably originated with the split-brain research of Roger Sperry in the 1960s.

The claim builds off this framework and suggests that people vary in how much they leverage each side of the brain.

THE APPEAL

The appeal is based upon noticeable differences in people. Some people are clearly capable of work in programing and science, for instance, while others are demonstrably artistic. If we can reliably attribute a person's capability to differences in which part of the brain they're better able to access, we have useful information.

THE POTENTIAL UPSIDE

If, indeed, we can be assessed based on the relative strengths of our brain hemispheres, we can either cater to an individual's strengths, or develop their areas of weakness. Similar to learning styles, we can adapt training with this knowledge. Further, we can use this information to help match people to careers.

THE POTENTIAL DOWNSIDE

If the differences between left and right brains aren't as clearly delineated, it means we're using a false basis upon which to characterize people. Moreover, people might self-limit based on a test.

HOW TO EVALUATE

One way to evaluate this claim is to use neural imaging data to see what happens in the brain for different people. Some differences in processing were suggested based on research where the corpus collosum of a patient was severed. (In these studies, the organ connecting the hemispheres was disconnected as a potential treatment for epilepsy.) At a neural level, however, the picture is complex.

We can gain some insight by looking more closely at functional magnetic resonance images (fMRI) of individuals, a technique that can map out brain connections. If we find that there are consistent separations of connections within the hemispheres, we can argue for lateralization. If the lateralization is only at a local level, and not systematic, we can infer that lateralization is not a consistent characteristic of individuals.

WHAT THE EVIDENCE SAYS

Looking at neuroimaging scans, researcher Jared A. Nielsen and colleagues (2013) analyzed images from a public data set to closely examine the lateralization of neurons. Contrary to the myth, they concluded that "our data are not consistent with a whole-brain phenotype of greater 'left-brained' or greater 'right-brained' network strength across individuals." Instead, they found lateralization in some areas, but not consistently in one individual versus another. In short, there's no evidence to support individuals being dominant in one hemisphere.

WHAT TO DO

We shouldn't pigeonhole people based on some test without a sound physiological basis. This is ultimately similar to the learning styles debate: We shouldn't bucket people by an artifact that doesn't withstand scrutiny. While the brain does exhibit some lateralization, it is still an incompletely understood organ, and despite individual variation it's too complex to simplify in this way.

Instead, we should be designing for the learning, not the learner.

CITATION

Nielsen, J.A., B.A. Zielinski, M.A. Ferguson, J.E. Lainhart, and J.S. Anderson. 2013. "An Evaluation of the Left-Brain vs. Right-Brain Hypothesis With Resting State Functional Connectivity Magnetic Resonance Imaging." *PLoS ONE* 8(8).

"I couldn't learn to think like a woman!"

MALE AND FEMALE DIFFERENCES IN LEARNING

THE CLAIM

Brain differences between men and women mean
we need to design learning differently for each.

Men's and women's brains differ, and so too then, according to this claim, should their learning. Women are more social and have better verbal memory. Men are better at spatial tasks. Therefore, we need to change how we design learning. We need to identify the ways in which the genders differ and then customize learning accordingly.

THE APPEAL

There are differences between men's and women's brains and in cognitive tasks. And, since they differ, there should be differences in processing. This ultimately means that we should accommodate those differences.

THE POTENTIAL UPSIDE

If we can reliably identify the brain differences between genders, then we should be able to identify the learning differences. If we can identify the learning differences, we can optimize training for the individual. This will respect the individual differences between genders, and give them unique opportunities to succeed.

THE POTENTIAL DOWNSIDE

If the differences aren't meaningful, we could waste money trying to adapt to a distinction that doesn't exist. We might design policies or programs that are ineffective at best, and detrimental at worst in the way they reinforce popularized stereotypes.

HOW TO EVALUATE

Brain scan technology has advanced to the point where researchers can very accurately scan the brains of men and women. And we have a sufficient catalog of such images that we can do a study across these brains and look at similarities and differences in considerable depth. From these studies, we can look at averages, and determine whether there are gender-related differences.

What these studies don't tell us is whether these differences influence learning. Thus, we have to determine whether or not there are learning differences. We may have to make inferences based upon theory.

WHAT THE EVIDENCE SAYS

Men's and women's brains do differ, on average, according to research by psychologist Daphna Joel and colleagues. That is, the distribution of differences in a variety of measures of the brain (grey matter, white matter, hippocampus, and so forth) are different. However, the individual differences in any one person's brain show more variation individually than they do with the average of the other gender. The overlap between the two genders is larger than the differences. As the researchers summarized: "Regardless of the cause of observed sex/gender differences in brain and behavior (nature or nurture), human brains cannot be categorized into two distinct classes: male brain/female brain" (Joel et al. 2015).

However, this does not inform us relative to learning. What is implied is that with the similarities noticed, we shouldn't choose to try to differentiate learning. If you can't categorize individuals by gender, you can't then categorize them for learning. It would require increasing the effort, for no obvious gain.

WHAT TO DO

Instead of designing for the learner, design for the knowledge. Use social learning not for gender reasons (for example, because women are more social), but because the negotiation of a shared understanding leads to a richer understanding. Don't use different media to appeal to different brains, do it because rich representations work for all learners (with caveats on overloading the essential elements). This also applies to workplace practices, such as having inclusive dialogue to appeal to women's preferences; do it because it's the right thing to do!

CITATION

Joel, D., Z. Berman, I. Tavor, N. Wexler, O. Gaber, Y. Stein, N. Shefi, J. Pool, S. Urchs, D.S. Margulies, F. Liem, J. Hanggi, L. Jancke, and Y. Assif. 2015. "Sex Beyond the Genitalia: The Human Brain Mosaic." *Proceedings of the National Academy of Sciences* 112(50).

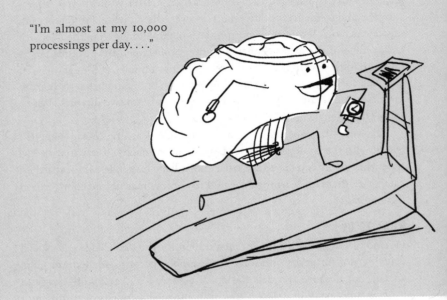

"I'm almost at my 10,000 processings per day. . . ."

BRAIN TRAINING

THE CLAIM

Regular brain training activities can improve
mental reasoning.

There was a flurry not that long ago of little games that supposedly improved your brain. They would have you look for patterns, remember things, and make inferences. These activities are designed to challenge you to solve problems of different sorts.

By regularly engaging in these activities, carefully chosen and balanced between tasks, you can improve your reasoning abilities. You'll be a better problem solver, and more!

THE APPEAL

If brain training works, we can improve our thinking. It's like going to the gym, but for the mind. Instead of becoming ripped, you get super smart!

The analogy with physical exercise is really what the claim is about. It is premised on an assumption that our brain benefits from exercise just as our body does.

THE POTENTIAL UPSIDE

If you can train your brain to be more effective, a bit of activity a day can give you a boost in your ability to work. You can be more intelligent about your life, which sounds like a big win. Just as the benefits of going to the gym increase your health, so too can you increase your smarts.

THE POTENTIAL DOWNSIDE

If brain training doesn't work, you could be wasting time and money. The money invested in the applications or workshops and the time taken to pursue these applications is gone with no return. You could be using your resources to better ends, such as learning specific things or accomplishing goals.

HOW TO EVALUATE

The best way to look at this myth is to look at studies that have evaluated brain training and see if they yielded positive outcomes, which is what psychologist Daniel J. Simons and others did. After a literature review, they found papers that met the minimum criteria for comparison, and then evaluated the overall outcomes.

Note the downside in attempting to evaluate brain-training games yourself: You might improve on similar tests, and there're reasons to think you will, but that improvement might not transfer to other areas. You'd need a test that was specific to your own daily tasks. While that's not impossible, it's certainly hard to do.

WHAT THE EVIDENCE SAYS

A detailed study by Simons and colleagues reviewing methodologies and results found no evidence that brain training yielded generalized improvements in brain function. While the training did improve the abilities that were trained, there was little transfer of improvement to near skills, and none to more general skills.

This isn't to say that there's no benefit: It seems like such activity, in lieu of other brain stimulation, can prolong cognitive function. That is, if you're older and relatively staid in your cognitive challenges, additional challenges can be beneficial.

However, for healthy adult employees, there's no obvious reason to engage. What does work is training on the specific mental skills needed. Or, in other words, training! Even meta-learning skills, such as learning to learn, are best practiced on top of existing tasks.

The old "learn Latin as exercise for the mind" has been proven false, and this really is no better.

WHAT TO DO

The right thing to do is to focus on developing the specific skills needed. If you need to train workers to troubleshoot systems, have them practice troubleshooting systems. If you need them to make better decisions with customers, practice making decisions with customers. The training can be simulated, but practicing specific skills is the way to get better at those skills. Unfortunately, there's no shortcut.

Similar to how learning styles pervade the industry, people and companies with a vested interest in brain training use narrow studies to suggest that their approach is valid. Yet when you get open and scrutable data and investigate them with an open mind, you'll find that there is no clear evidence to invest in these new approaches.

CITATION

Simons, D.J., W.R. Boot, N. Charness, S.E. Gathercole, C.F. Chabris, D.Z. Hambrick, and E.A. Stine-Morrow. 2016. "Do 'Brain-Training' Programs Work?" *Psychological Science in the Public Interest* 17(3): 103-186.

"My brain
goes up to 11!"

10 PERCENT OF OUR BRAIN

THE CLAIM

Humans use only 10 percent of their brain.

There's a persistent belief that humans use only 10 percent of their brain. That is, we've enormous capacity, but much of it is untapped. If only we could tap some proportion of that available capability!

The origin seems to come from a statement by the early and eminent psychologist William James, who claimed we weren't fully taking advantage of our potential. It also may come from studies that show not all of our brain is active at any one time. This certainly resonates.

THE APPEAL

Not fully using our brains would explain a number of things: why some people are smarter than others, why we can continue to learn, why we can't levitate that book, and more. It would be a shame to miss out on so much; if there's untapped potential, there's an opportunity to become better as a species.

THE POTENTIAL UPSIDE

If we know that we're using only 10 percent of our brains, there's a strong belief that we can tap into that remaining 90 percent of capability. We can be smarter, and consequently we can be more successful.

THE POTENTIAL DOWNSIDE

If, in fact, we don't use only 10 percent of our brain (or we do, but we are unable to improve upon that), we might be wasting time trying to pursue efforts to improve our brain utilization.

HOW TO EVALUATE

You can evaluate this claim in several ways. One would be to learn how the brain actually works, and discover that full utilization might not make sense. Another would be to use brain scans to determine how much of the brain is being used. Each of these can provide insight. We might also look at the energy utilization of the brain, or results from studies of brain damage, but the first two are sufficient.

WHAT THE EVIDENCE SAYS

The brain is composed of many neurons, and activity (such as thinking) is distributed across it. Consequently, any concept is a pattern of activation across less than the full brain. Other concepts are other patterns. Thus, at any one moment we might be using 10 percent of our brains, but we'd be using different parts, and it's shifting continuously. Thus, we're using the full brain, just different parts at different times, and that's of necessity.

While there's no specific study to cite here, journalist Robynne Boyd went directly to neuroscientists to address this myth. She was told that many different parts of the brain are active all the time. Even when we're sleeping, many different parts of the brain are active. In total, 100 percent of the brain is used throughout the day.

So, the short answer is that you're not going to be able to tap into more brain power, except by the old-fashioned ways of continually learning. The ways we're not effective in using the brain appropriately have to do with our investment of time, not in accessing unused portions. We can do better, but it comes from effort, not availability.

WHAT TO DO

When you want to increase your ability to do something, learn it, practice it, perform it. There are no shortcuts.

CITATION

Boyd, R. 2008. "Do People Only Use 10% of Their Brains?" *Scientific American,* February 8. www.scientificamerican.com/article/do-people-only-use-10-percent-of-their-brains.

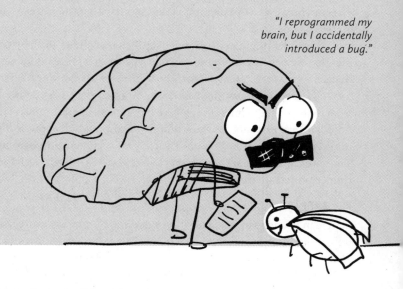

"I reprogrammed my brain, but I accidentally introduced a bug."

NEURO-LINGUISTIC PROGRAMMING

THE CLAIM

We can improve our behavior through neuro-linguistic programming initiatives based upon language and action.

We all recognize that our actions aren't always ideal. We respond to situations where, upon reflection, we could have handled them better. The claim with neuro-linguistic programming, or NLP, is that we can improve our behavior by reprogramming our neurological systems.

The basis of neuro-linguistic programming is that our interpretation of the world isn't exactly coherent with the actual world. As a consequence, our existing patterns of understanding and action may represent misapprehensions. The premise is that by changing the patterns, we can better respond.

The model, originated in the 1970s by Richard Bandler and John Grinder, says that we perceive the world through a primary representational system that combines to different degrees the five senses: visual, kinesthetic, auditory, olfactory, and gustatory. Moreover, a trained expert can detect signals from that system, such as through eye movements (neuro), understand our "map" or interpretation of the world from how we talk about it (linguistic), and reprogram it through a variety of techniques (programming). Thus, we can personally be changed to be effective through the efforts of a trained professional.

THE APPEAL

If we can change our behavior in positive ways—improve our behavior—we can be more successful. The appeal, then, is that with a systematic approach, based upon rigorous work, we can reliably achieve these ends. If we can detect our models and reprogram our behaviors, we can react in more useful and appropriate ways.

The originators studied recognized therapists and created a formal structure that represented what they believed was happening. The formalization implied further methods that could be incorporated into the overall approach to create a rich framework for solutions. This implies a rich potential for successful improvement.

THE POTENTIAL UPSIDE

The upside is broader than personal improvement. If, at an organizational level, we can bring in or train people to apply this approach, we can improve the workforce. We can leverage a competitive advantage in our employee's improved behavior. In addition, as employees become more effective, they will attribute that improvement to the organization. We can identify a person's map, document problems, and apply specific revisions—sometimes as quickly as a single session.

THE POTENTIAL DOWNSIDE

If neuro-linguistic programming doesn't work, we could be encouraging our organizations to invest in an approach that can't achieve the results we need. Further, we could delude ourselves that we are effecting meaningful change, yet without basis. We could further wrongly promulgate beliefs in, and investments of, our employees in these areas.

HOW TO EVALUATE

Given how long the neuro-linguistic programming concept has been around, and the years of studies into its effectiveness, the best way to evaluate this claim is to conduct a meta-analysis. Here, we can analyze published research and evaluate the findings. By sorting through studies to find ones with sufficient rigor and evaluate the results, we can determine whether there's a sound analytical basis.

WHAT THE EVIDENCE SAYS

In 2011 Tomasz Witkowski, a psychologist at the University of Wroclaw in Poland, reviewed a wide variety of research from an online database of the NLP Community, a Germany-based group in support of the concept. Conducting a rigorous analysis, he found 33 empirical studies that had sufficient relevance and rigor. Of them, the studies that supported NLP were outnumbered roughly two to one by nonsupportive studies (another smaller segment of the studies was ambiguous). Witkowski's results make clear that there's no validity to the claims for NLP effectiveness; arguments against the theoretical components exist, too.

Other works reflect the same questionable basis. Witkowski refers to previous studies, such as the 1987 paper by Christopher Sharpley, a research professor in neuroscience at the University of New England in Australia, which concluded that "research data do not support either the basic tenets of NLP or their application in counseling situations." Similarly, psychologist Gareth Roderique Davies (2009) wrote, "after three decades, there is still no credible theoretical basis for NLP." The neuro-linguistic programming approach fails on both empirical and conceptual grounds.

WHAT TO DO

Behavior is often not as optimal as we would like, and we do have ways to change it. However, those approaches tend to work on other bases than neuro-linguistic programming. Cognitive behavioral therapy, for instance, is a research-based practice that works along similar lines of looking at a person's beliefs versus what's real, and addressing those. And it doesn't do it through "magic" approaches, but through sustained work on reframing beliefs.

Moreover, if you want to change specific behaviors, you use training. Not just a one-time event, but a sustained learning program that provides sufficient contextualized practice, resourced with models and examples, to establish the desired behavior. The program should progress from practice through coached performance, and participants should leave as members of an ongoing community of like-minded practitioners.

CITATIONS

Roderique Davies, G. 2009. "Neuro Linguistic Programming: Cargo Cult Psychology?" *Journal of Applied Research in Higher Education* 1(2): 58-63.

Sharpley, C.F. 1987. "Research Findings on Neurolinguistic Programming: Nonsupportive Data or an Untestable Theory?" *Journal of Counseling Psychology* 4(1): 103-107.

Witkowski, T. 2011. "Thirty-Five Years of Research on Neuro-Linguistic Programming. NLP Research Data Base. State of the Art or Pseudoscientific Decoration?" *Polish Psychological Bulletin* 41(2): 58-66.

"I don't know
what to do now;
I never failed in
practice."

ERROR-FREE LEARNING

THE CLAIM

Making mistakes is not useful for learning.

There's something intuitive about this claim. After all, how can making mistakes be beneficial to learning? It would make learning take longer, reinforce wrong answers, and even affect the learner's emotional state. The focus on no mistakes goes back to the days of behaviorism in the 1930s. Researchers such as psychologist B.F. Skinner believed that reinforcing only the right answers kept us from strengthening the links to wrong answers. There was a call for error-free or errorless learning. This is coupled with a belief that it's rude, or cruel, to have learners fail.

Overall, you will find folks who either make the question easy, or provide so much guidance about the right answer that a learner would have to work hard to get it wrong. You've probably seen the quiz questions where the alternatives to the right answer are so silly or obvious that you'd have to try hard to actually fail. They're ubiquitous.

THE APPEAL

Making no mistakes on the journey to learning has two appeals. For one, it seems most effective. If we're not making mistakes, we're not wasting time getting the feedback on what went wrong and then having to get it right the next time around. Second, it's more pleasurable. We don't like to make mistakes, and we could affect the learner's self-esteem if we support letting them fail.

THE POTENTIAL UPSIDE

We can infer two upsides to error-free learning. For one, we should be able to optimize the learning experience, reinforcing only the necessary right answers. And we can maintain our learner's self-image as effective learners and performers.

THE POTENTIAL DOWNSIDE

If mistakes are valuable to the learning process, we might undermine our learning goals by avoiding mistakes at all costs. Our outcomes might not be robust. That's for the specific domains, but we might also undermine learners' abilities to deal with real problems, such as being able to reassess and rectify, if they have no experience with errors.

HOW TO EVALUATE

There has been a considerable amount of research on errors in learning. An obvious way, then, is to review the literature and create a synthesis that makes sense of disparate outcomes. A second approach would be a causal story of the processes associated with making mistakes and learning from them.

WHAT THE EVIDENCE SAYS

The research, as reviewed by psychologist Janet Metcalfe, says that in most instances, making mistakes improves learning outcomes. For example, choosing an alternative that represents a common misconception and getting feedback about why that's not right decreases the likelihood that you'll make that mistake in an actual performance situation. However, this comes with a caveat: With good feedback! When people make mistakes and can learn from them, the outcomes are better. (As an interesting aside, people learn more from mistakes the more they were certain they were correct!)

There's a broader argument here: The ability to learn from mistakes carries over beyond the specific domain. There are cognitive skills involved in processing the difference between the learner's choice and the right answer. Those are skills that can and should be developed as well, creating resilience. Similarly, the ability to accept that mistakes are okay as long as the lesson is learned is a valuable mindset for success.

Note that just seeing a question and then seeing the answer (such as with a rollover) isn't sufficient. The learners need to process the question and select an answer for the feedback to be relevant.

In fact, not providing a sufficient challenge—by making the question or problem so obvious, for example—can make the learning take longer, and keep learners from having to make difficult discriminations. Doing so might even put your organization at a disadvantage as, increasingly, challenging decisions are likely to be the success differentiator for organizations.

There are situations where error-free learning is useful, to be sure. Individuals with brain damage have trouble with the necessary cognitive overhead to process mistakes, but this is also largely in the role of low-level learnings.

WHAT TO DO

Make problems for learners sufficiently challenging, so that they must actively engage cognitive processes to succeed. The alternatives to the right answer should represent plausible ways learners can go wrong. You may have to start with more simple discriminations initially to keep the challenge within bounds, but you'll want to ramp it up as the learners' abilities increase.

Make sure the feedback provides a rich basis for learners to comprehend why their response was wrong and correct their mistakes. Refer to the rationale that guides performance, and point out how they violated the appropriate reasoning.

It's also important to make it safe to make mistakes. Even if the consequences for failure in performance are harsh, the environment for learning should have the harshness in the challenge, not in the learning consequences.

CITATION

Metcalfe, J. 2017. "Learning From Errors." *Annual Review of Psychology* 68.

"But what happens if there're both images and text?"

IMAGES ARE 60,000 TIMES BETTER THAN TEXT

THE CLAIM

People process images 60,000 times faster than text.

When there's a choice to be made to communicate using text or images, the claim has been that images are the better option. Advocates point to research that shows people process images significantly faster than text. The claim has been made in a variety of guises, most frequently for marketing and advertisements, but for learning as well.

THE APPEAL

Our brains are very visual: We have more brain space allocated for processing vision than auditory input, for instance. And we all have heard the statement "a picture is worth a thousand words," which originated in advertising. We were also effectively dealing with the world long before we invented text. Thus, there's a strong argument that we should be biased toward processing images more easily than text.

THE POTENTIAL UPSIDE

If the claim for image precedence is true, we should use images whenever possible to communicate more effectively. We can support cognitive processing efficiencies, yielding quicker outcomes.

THE POTENTIAL DOWNSIDE

If, in fact, we don't process images faster, we might erroneously use images when they're not going to help. We might design learning that makes it harder for the learner to comprehend the message, and thereby undermine the effectiveness of our designs.

HOW TO EVALUATE

In this case, it's important to find the research from which this myth originated, if it exists. Once we see the original research, we can evaluate the legitimacy of the claim. If such a search results in a dead end, we have to question the claim.

We can also make a determination based on some cognitive reasoning. We know our sensory memory is remarkably fast, so if text processing must be actively engaged in working memory, and images aren't, we could

. substantiate a claim of such a difference. If, however, they ultimately need the same mechanisms, there's a case that such a difference is implausible.

WHAT THE EVIDENCE SAYS

Uncovering the original research has been the subject of considerable effort, not least from Alan Levine. He's even put up money to find the original research. The claim appears to have been made in a presentation from a 3M company employee around 2000. However, despite some claims that it came from internal research, no one has been able to find the study. Consistent effort by others confirms the challenge in documenting the origin of the claim.

Cognitively speaking, our visual inputs are captured in sensory store, and then what we pay attention to is processed by working memory. However, anything familiar enough can bypass the working memory stage and be recognized. And, indeed, there is evidence of very rapid image processing. However, words are visual representations too, and any word familiar enough will similarly benefit from recognition.

WHAT TO DO

Images are valuable, when they convey related information. Additional information that's not germane can actually interfere with learning. The appropriate use of media is governed by its cognitive properties. There are times when images work best, such as when you want to convey context, and times when text works better, such as conveying abstract concepts. Using the right media for the job is a better principle than simply using images indiscriminately.

CITATION

Levine, A. 2016. "Stop the Madness: The Proliferation of the 60000 Times Faster Myth Dances On." Cog Dog Blog, May 1. http://cogdogblog .com/2016/05/stop-the-madness.

PEOPLE DON'T NEED KNOWLEDGE

THE CLAIM

People don't need knowledge, only skills.

The claim is that providing people with practice on skills to perform some task will provide a sufficient basis for the ability to do it. (This is the flip side of the learning design belief that providing knowledge is sufficient.) The claim implies that if you develop the skills, you naturally develop the knowledge, and there's no need to focus on the knowledge separately. There's a persistent belief in the value of general problem-solving skills. Being able to recite facts isn't as important as the ability to make decisions.

THE APPEAL

It's clear that what matters is the ability to do, not just know. Therefore, focusing on developing the ability to do should define the extent of our efforts. If we provide people with sufficient practice on the skills, they will be able to transfer those skills appropriately.

THE POTENTIAL UPSIDE

If indeed we don't need knowledge, we can do away with all the content presentation that accompanies our learning. We can strip the focus down to a series of practice activities with feedback. We can eliminate the knowledge dump that characterizes so much of learning activities.

THE POTENTIAL DOWNSIDE

If knowledge is valuable, but we deemphasize it to focus only on practice, we might leave learners ill equipped to actually succeed. Instead, we have to work hard to determine the knowledge required and ensure it's provided. We still want to minimize the amount of knowledge shared to what's valuable, so we have to be discriminating. We know that experts can't access all they do, but they do have access to all they learned and know, so they'll err on the side of content presentation. And content presentation can be uninvolving. We have to strike the right balance.

HOW TO EVALUATE

One way to evaluate this claim is to summarize the research on knowledge across a wide variety of performance situations. If we find research that clearly demonstrates the value of knowledge in developing skills, we can counter this belief. If, on the other hand, we don't find such research, and instead see that the development of skills alone suffices to lead to transferable expertise, we can maintain our faith that knowledge isn't needed.

A second way would be to look at what's required to develop cognitive skills. If a rigorous and successful learning design approach works by focusing on skills without knowledge, we can maintain a belief that knowledge isn't important. If, on the other hand, the design approach points to a combined focus on knowledge and skills together, we should believe that they are coupled together.

WHAT THE EVIDENCE SAYS

The evidence shows very clearly that knowledge provides a framework to develop first an inflexible, and then a flexible, ability to apply that knowledge to solve meaningful problems. Psychologist Daniel T. Willingham covers a robust series of research studies that point to the importance of knowledge in developing skills. Included are research on such representative skills as chess, and meta-analyses across a wide variety of studies to improve science problem solving, where the best methods involve improving students' knowledge.

Similarly, scholar Jeroen Van Merriënboer's Four-Component Instructional Design approach does away with the detailed structure of Bloom's Taxonomy, and focuses on two things: the knowledge required and the skills to apply that knowledge to complex problems. Typically, the most complex skills are the most valuable as well, so such a learning design process should be the most relevant. As this design includes a focus on knowledge, we can infer that there's a valuable role for knowledge in the overall success.

WHAT TO DO

Skills are the necessary outcome we want, but knowledge is critical to developing skills that are transferable to the necessary situations. Too much knowledge without application isn't likely to be remembered, but too much practice without knowledge development leads to insufficient flexibility in application. Knowledge development moves from rote to inflexible to flexible, so it's important to develop the knowledge and skills together. Bringing in the knowledge at the point of application makes it relevant.

CITATIONS

Willingham, D.T. 2006. "How Knowledge Helps: It Speeds and Strengthens Reading Comprehension, Learning—and Thinking." *American Educator* 1:30.

Van Merriënboer, J.J.G. 1997. *Training Complex Cognitive Skills: A Four-Component Instructional Design Model for Technical Training.* Englewood Cliffs, NJ: Educational Technology Publications.

LEARNING SUPERSTITIONS

Superstitions around learning aren't propagated as explicit claims about what people should do, so much as they are prevalent practices that persist despite their lack of value. And such beliefs can influence decisions in terms of products to support learning design or the learning design itself. They may be embodied in the feature suite of authoring tools or emerge in practice. In either case, if they're not valuable, they're wasted effort and lead to bad design.

Many learning superstitions are driven by expediency. It appears that when we try to accomplish the holy trinity of product creation (fast, cheap, and good), the reality usually ends up as a "pick two" compromise erring on the side of fast and cheap. When a designer is presented with content files and expected to work in timeframes for course creation on the order of days, that's creating unrealistic expectations.

This section calls out a representative selection of these superstitions, covering most of the problems and explaining why they can't be real. This isn't to say anyone's explicitly saying "Do this," but these superstitions are widespread in learning design. And they're bad practice.

Seriously, these practices violate known properties of our brains, and we should be professional enough to push back against requests that lead us to err in these ways. Here, I hope to give you the ammunition you need to avoid these steps.

"But I've told them it's bad!?!?"

PRESENTATION = ACQUISITION

THE CLAIM

If you've covered it, they've learned it.

THE PRACTICE

The mantra, popularized by Harold Stolovitch, is that "telling ain't training." Yet we've all experienced the alternative; someone's presented you with a bunch of bullet points about what you're supposed to do, and that's it! There's an implicit belief that if you've seen it, it is good. But is it?

THE RATIONALE

The rationale behind this practice is that our audiences are smart, and as long as they have the information, they'll be able to apply it. They simply have to remember the information in the right context, and then it'll be obvious how to use that information to succeed.

Or we might go a half-step further and present a few examples showing the information in action. These examples will make it easier for the learners to remember the topic, while also providing a reference during the situation.

WHY IT DOESN'T WORK

For learners to remember something, they need to practice remembering it in situations like those in which they'll be using it. In *Make It Stick,* summarizing the results of considerable research, Peter Brown and co-authors point out that retrieval practice is required for true proficiency. That is, to retrieve the knowledge in context, learners need to practice retrieving (and using) the information in situations that are close enough to those they'll see in the performance environment.

In cognitive science, we talk about "inert knowledge": you can recite it, but when it's relevant in context it doesn't even get activated, let alone applied. Even if we know the information well enough to recite it for a test, it's not only unlikely to be available later, it's unlikely to be activated even if it *is* available.

WHAT TO DO INSTEAD

Focus on what learners need to practice first, and then develop the content around that baseline (and specifically models and examples). Cathy Moore's action mapping technique, codified in her 2017 book *Map It,* is a nice heuristic way to think about design: Figure out what your learners have to be able to do, create a practice situation where they have to do it, and then provide only the resources (read: content) necessary for them to succeed. Note that if the final task is complex enough, you're going to need a series of practice activities.

CITATIONS

Brown, P.C., H.L. Roediger, and M.A. McDaniel. 2014. *Make It Stick: The Science of Successful Learning.* Cambridge, MA: Belknap Press.

Moore, C. 2017. *Map It: The Hands-On Guide to Strategic Training Design.* Montesa Press.

"But I passed the quiz!"

KNOWLEDGE TEST = LEARNING OUTCOME

THE CLAIM

If they can recite it, they can do it.

THE PRACTICE

How often have you seen an e-learning module that's basically content and a quiz? That's emblematic of a design that boils down to a presentation of information and then a knowledge assessment to test some representative subset of the material. And that's when it's done well; sometimes the test questions touch on obscure and irrelevant pieces or material that isn't even covered in the course. The assessment might consist of several quizzes scattered throughout or one at the end.

More often than not, the test questions are about knowledge recall. They're not testing how to apply the knowledge, just whether you can recite it. And, typically, it's one question on any one thing, which is insufficient practice.

THE RATIONALE

While there are several reasons why this practice pervades adult learning courses and programs, it ultimately comes back to how material was taught in school, where you studied textbooks and recited the knowledge back during a test. There's a familiarity with the process that makes it appealing. And, after all, it worked, right? (Not likely.)

Another rationale is that this design is what authoring tools are largely oriented toward: Put content in and design a quiz for the content. We can easily convert PowerPoint files and PDFs into screens and add some questions. When we're rushed for time or otherwise interested in churning out multiple learning programs quickly, this is about as simple as it gets.

It's also easier to write assessments, particularly ones that are auto-marked, that are knowledge based. You can even get artificial intelligence software that will process a body of knowledge as text and not only be able to answer questions, but also generate them.

WHY IT DOESN'T WORK

While having an assessment is a good step to incorporate in your learning design, it's usually not enough. Sure, if you need to train people to recite certain knowledge, like product information or rote responses, this approach can work. But it's not guaranteed. That's because to ensure a modicum of learning transfer, the knowledge recitation has to be tested several times, spaced over several days, not just once after the completion of the course. Overall, this approach is overworked.

Even in recitation circumstances, people typically need the knowledge of how to use it, as well as opportunities to put it to use. They need to counter customer objections, diagnose system problems, and calculate prices and commissions. Just reciting the knowledge in an assessment isn't going to lead to the ability to do.

It turns out that to solve problems, people need to practice solving problems. And these problems should be concrete examples, not abstract ones—contextualized problems, in settings like the ones they will face.

Our brains are wired to develop the connections that are used. If we're used to reciting knowledge without context, we're unlikely to be able to do it when applicable in a particular context. And if we've never used knowledge to solve problems, we're unlikely to be able to when the time comes.

WHAT TO DO INSTEAD

Give learners tasks to use what they've learned that mirror how they'll use it after the learning experience. Have them perform it like they'll need to perform in the real world.

Note that this doesn't necessarily mean simulations or branching scenarios, although those are both great approaches. It can even be just better written multiple-choice questions. I argue as much in my book on designing learning experiences, *Engaging Learning,* where you use mini scenarios to present a situation. For each question, the choices represent actions to be taken as a result of decisions made, and the alternatives represent misconceptions.

CITATION

Quinn, C. 2005. *Engaging Learning: Designing e-Learning Simulation Games.* San Francisco: Pfieffer.

"Why are there so many clicks needed?"

INTERACTION = ENGAGEMENT

THE CLAIM

Interactions like clicking are intrinsically interesting.

THE PRACTICE

Designers are frequently told to "make it more interactive." The result? They create many different types of interactions that reflect a desire to get a learner to "act to see more," such as "click to reveal more" or "rollover to see the answer."

THE RATIONALE

It's all part of a belief that to keep learners engaged, you need to keep them active. Just clicking to advance isn't enough, they need to do more. So, if we put extra activities on (at least some of) the pages, it'll be more interesting. Learners won't be passive, they'll be active!

In our attempt to drive this active participation, we create a variety of interactions to insert that have one core function: It reveals more information after they take an action. It can be a swipe, a drag, a click, or even a rollover. And more variety should be even more engaging!

WHY IT DOESN'T WORK

The problem is, interaction doesn't equal application or engagement. If we're asking learners to click multiple times, all we're doing is having them interact to access more content. It's fundamentally no different than clicking to the next page. Sure, we can use the spatial layout to convey more information as well, but it's still just content presentation.

Engagement comes from either a cognitive challenge or an intrinsic interest. If you're telling a story, clicking to reveal the hiccups or resolution is like reading a book and turning the pages. If you've got to commit to a choice before seeing the consequences, your brain has to actively process the information.

Initially, you might get a slight increase in user attention with these activities, but they'll quickly pale. You want intrinsic motivation, and these actions are extrinsic. In fact, gratuitous interactions can actually increase cognitive load and interfere with learning.

WHAT TO DO INSTEAD

Punctuate your content with meaningful interactions. First, trim out any unnecessary content. Is the information going to make a difference in their ability to make the right decision? If not, throw it out. Do they already know it, at least well enough? Then scrap it.

Then, have them apply the knowledge. Ask them a question, drag and drop words to create a hierarchy, or have them do something with the knowledge. Don't show them more—have them use what you've already said.

"But they all loved my swimming lessons!"

"Help!"

SMILE SHEETS = EVALUATION

THE CLAIM

If they like it, it is effective.

THE PRACTICE

When evaluating learning (if it's done at all), we too often rely on asking the learners to evaluate the session. Colloquially known as a "smile sheet" (in that people can indicate their happiness with a face representing a smile, neutral, or a frown), this type of evaluation is a frequently seen component of training. The point is to use the learner's evaluations of the learning experience as a metric to determine the quality of the learning experience. Trainers and designers are then evaluated for their abilities based upon learner feedback.

THE RATIONALE

The simple rationale is that organizations believe that if they're doing Level 1, they're at least making a start on evaluation. It may not be the whole picture, but at least something is being done.

And going beyond smile sheets is hard; that's why so many learning departments don't go further. (In a 2016 study titled *Evaluating Learning*, ATD found that 92 percent of organizations were evaluating at Level 1, but the numbers dropped off from there.) Creating a separate assessment can be difficult to administer in the classroom. It's not fun! The next step—looking for changed behavior—might mean having to go in and talk to the relevant business units and getting permission or asking managers to do extra work.

Looking at data for the learning impact, well, that's just too hard. That requires getting access to real data and tracking them. And then what would we do with it? It's not like we're going to go back and change the training program; we've got new courses to design and deliver.

WHY IT DOESN'T WORK

The simple problem is that a learner's assessment of learning isn't a good indicator of the actual quality of the learning experience. Most people will rate a pleasurable course more favorably than one that challenges them because the latter requires them to actually think. In fact, a 1997 study conducted by George M. Alliger and other researchers suggested that there was about zero correlation between learner assessment of the quality of the learning experience and the actual outcomes (0.09, which is zero with a rounding error).

Quite simply, under most circumstances subjective experience isn't a great indicator of learning impact. Unless your learners are relative experts in pedagogy or the domain, they're going to be unlikely to accurately evaluate the outcomes. A positive affect isn't a good indicator of a positive impact!

WHAT TO DO INSTEAD

In *Performance-Focused Smile Sheets,* Will Thalheimer suggests ways to modify the process to obtain meaningful results, which includes conducting the evaluation some period after the learning experience ends. In the broader perspective, we could refer to the Kirkpatrick Model (Kirkpatrick and Kirkpatrick 2016), where the subjective learner evaluation is referred to as Level 1, and goes on from there. Level 2 is assessing learner competency after the learning experience, Level 3 is looking for actual change in workplace behavior, and Level 4 is looking for impact on business outcomes. And, of course, starting with Level 4 and working backward! After all, meaningful course design should have a goal of influencing some measurable gap.

CITATIONS

Alliger, G.M., S.I. Tannenbaum, W. Bennett Jr, H. Traver, and A. Shotland. 1997. "A Meta-Analysis of the Relations Among Training Criteria." *Personnel Psychology* 50(2): 341-358.

ATD (Association for Talent Development). 2016. *Evaluating Learning: Getting to Measurements That Matter.* Alexandria, VA: ATD Press.

Kirkpatrick, J.D., and W.K. Kirkpatrick. 2016. *Kirkpatrick's Four Levels of Training Evaluation.* ATD Press: Alexandria, VA.

Thalheimer, W. 2016. *Performance-Focused Smile Sheets: A Radical Rethinking of a Dangerous Art Form.* Work-Learning Press: Somerville, MA.

LEARNING SHOULD BE
EASY OR HARD

THE CLAIM

Learning needs to be either really hard (to actually
work) or really easy (so learners don't feel bad).

THE PRACTICE

Too often, practice items are designed to be either ridiculously easy or frustratingly hard. The former is more prevalent than the latter, but both can be seen (although typically not together). For example, we see multiple-choice questions where the alternatives to the right answer are either silly or obvious.

THE RATIONALE

On the one hand, there is a belief that learning should be easy. People talk about making learning engaging, and if it's hard it can't be fun, right? If we can make learners laugh, they'll better connect with the content—and maybe even give us a better rating on our smile sheet (see Smile Sheets = Evaluation). There's another belief about learners' self-esteem that also drives making it easy. The concern is that if learners fail, their confidence will shatter. We don't want them dropping out of the learning experience because they don't think they're capable.

On the other hand is the belief that learning should be hard work. That is, if learners know they need to work to succeed, they'll invest the effort and learn more. One of the manifestations of this are questions asking for minute trivia about the content. These questions act more as "gotchas" than as true attempts at assessing learning transfer. Alternatively, the discriminations between the answers to choose from are so detailed as to be almost impenetrable.

WHY IT DOESN'T WORK

From several perspectives, we see that there are productive zones for determining problem difficulty. In learning, we can point to psychologist Lev Vygotsky's Zone of Proximal Development. Vygotsky notes that there are tasks within the learner's grasp, and tasks beyond the learner no matter how much support is available. In between is the place where learning can happen, where learners can diligently learn.

In engagement, psychologist Mihaly Csikszentmihalyi documented the zone of appropriate challenge—below it are tasks too easy and consequently boring, and above it are tasks too difficult and frustrating. This suggests that there's a "sweet spot" between too hard and too easy where learning happens.

You can also look at the behavioral curve of the Yerkes-Dodson law, named after psychologists Robert M. Yerkes and John Dillingham Dodson. Through their research they graphed individual performance against the level of challenge (formally referred to as "arousal"). They found that a moderate level of challenge leads to better performance, but too little or too much will decrease performance.

From the point of learning, these perspectives align perfectly— learning can and should be "hard fun." Further, the zone changes as the learner progresses. The acceptable challenge increases as the learner's abilities progress. The point is that the extreme ends of the learning challenge aren't helpful, and there's an appropriate level of challenge to be addressed.

If we've done a good enough job of motivating learners in the first place, they should persist through some failure, particularly if the feedback makes it clear it's about the decision, not the learner.

WHAT TO DO INSTEAD

The right thing to do is to calibrate the challenge to the learners' abilities— make a challenge that is within their reach, but not necessarily within their grasp. You need to start with appropriate discriminations for their level of ability, then adjust as they internalize the basics.

You ultimately may need learners to be able to make extremely challenging discriminations, just try to avoid them at the beginning. Instead, start with simpler discriminations, such as using less factors or simpler numbers, or solving part of the problem for them.

The right alternative to the wrong answer is not something random or silly, but ways they reliably go wrong in practice. You want to identify their misconceptions, and make those choices possible in the learning situation, where you can address it—and before it happens when it counts.

CITATIONS

Csikszentmihalyi, M., and I.S. Csikszentmihalyi. 1988. *Optimal Experience: Psychological Studies of Flow in Consciousness.* New York: Cambridge University Press.

Vygotsky, L.S. 1978. *Mind in Society.* Edited by M. Cole, V. John-Steiner, S. Scribner, and E. Souberman. Cambridge, MA: Harvard University Press.

Yerkes, R.M., and J.D. Dodson. 1908. "The Relation of Strength of Stimulus to Rapidity of Habit-Formation." *Journal of Comparative Neurology and Psychology* 18:459-482.

LEARNING MISCONCEPTIONS

Now that we've covered the learning myths and superstitions, let's dive into a category of approaches that are more controversial. In these topics, some folks claim they're myths, but others are fervent advocates. The differences are not about the data, but about the interpretation. These confusions keep us from making the best decisions about design. Here, the goal is to create understandings that rule out the problems and provide useful recommendations.

In this section, we'll lay out the claim and the appeal, present the counter arguments, and create a reconciliation that provides an integrative framework. This then leads us to useful practices.

To be sure, this reconciliation will not remove the controversy. There are smart people on both sides of the argument. They may not agree with my interpretation, or might argue that what I'm doing is changing the framework. My goal is to help people create practical and valuable solutions, and I'm quite comfortable taking an interpretation that gives us leverage even if it's not completely pure.

Note that this is different from just playing fast and loose with the facts. I will not violate any known science to make my interpretations. Instead, I'll separate out what's false from what's useful. In this section, you're free to disagree with my interpretation. (That said, I'm confident you'll be hard-pressed to disagree with the recommendations!)

Again, what follows are my interpretations to help get the best out of some ideas while avoiding interpretations that can lead you astray. Not all will agree, but hopefully you will find this useful.

"But the numbers are wrong."

"It's not about the numbers."

"But the numbers are wrong."

"IT'S NOT ABOUT THE #$^&*[NUMBERS!"

"BUT THE NUMBERS ARE WRONG!"

70-20-10

THE CLAIM

70-20-10 is a useful framework to help people design better performance solutions.

Back in the 1970s, the Center for Creative Leadership asked leaders where they learned their leadership skills. On average, the numbers roughly showed that they learned 10 percent of what they used from courses, 20 percent from coaching and social interactions, and 70 percent from experimentation. Further research has validated the notion that people in other tasks report a similar distribution of how they developed their skills. Jay Cross, in an appendix to his landmark book *Informal Learning,* points to a wide variety of studies that show informal learning ranging from 70 to 90 percent.

This research has led proponents—most prominently Charles Jennings, co-founder of the 70-20-10 Institute—to suggest that using a framework of projects or assignments and coaching to complement formal learning is a useful and necessary adjunct to courses. They argue that it's not about the numbers, it's just a way to help people get their minds around going beyond training.

With fellow co-founders Jos Arets and Vivian Heijnen, Jennings also applies the framework to an overall performance perspective that includes job aids and courses.

THE COUNTER

Opponents of 70-20-10 argue that the numbers aren't validated by empirical research. (It's even listed in *Urban Myths About Learning and Education,* by educational scientists Pedro De Bruyckere, Paul A. Kirschner, and Casper Hulshof.) As we've discussed with several other myths in this book, you never get such clear numbers from research. And, what research has been conducted has produced widely varying results.

The argument is that this framework isn't research based, and consequently isn't a sound basis for designing workplace learning. Instead, we should follow sound, evidence-based principles when designing extensions to courses, such as the need for spaced practice, coaching, and so on.

Their conclusion? This model is a proprietary model with vested interests, which isn't soundly based and should be avoided.

RECONCILIATION

While it's true that the numbers aren't exact, the flip side is that most learning solution designs fail to go beyond the course. If we instead use the principles of 70-20-10 as a rough guideline, we can gain value from it, but learning design professionals aren't doing so.

In *702010: Towards 100% Performance,* Arets, Jennings, and Heijnen are clearly focused on designing solutions as a mix of performance support, courses, coaching, and stretch assignments, not on relying on the numbers alone. Thanks to several different roles, detailed steps in breaking things down, and successful examples and workshops, their 70-20-10 model is helping learning designers get success. And that's the real and important empirical result.

Moreover, Jennings has found that this model works to sensitize executives to thinking beyond the course. Most executives have gone to school, and yet they aren't learning experts. Thus, they're inclined, without guided introspection, to consider that professional learning can look like school and resist using any resources to go beyond the course. Using this framework, however, Jennings has helped organizations switch to a more appropriate investment of resources, yielding higher outcomes.

WHAT TO DO

Let me be clear: Charles Jennings is a friend and colleague of mine. However, I have no financial stake in 70-20-10 and my reputation as an independent arbiter is at risk. While I have no reason to misconstrue my interpretation, take my recommendation with the proverbial grain of salt.

My recommendation is that you use 70-20-10 if it's of use to you. If you have trouble getting people in your organization to let you start working on a performance consulting approach or using extended models of organizational learning, 70-20-10 can help. It's a quick tool to help executives reflect on their own learning (such as, "How much of what you do did you learn through courses?").

If you've already gotten leverage to start working on programs that extend the learning experience across time, with spacing and facilitation, you likely don't need 70-20-10. Similarly, if you are doing performance consulting and creating solutions that focus on meaningful outcomes, you're not likely in need.

CITATIONS

Arets, J., C. Jennings, and V. Heijnen. 2016. *702010: Towards 100% Performance.* Maastricht, NL: Sutler Media.

Cross, J. 2007. *Informal Learning: Rediscovering the Natural Pathways That Inspire Innovation and Performance.* San Francisco: Pfeiffer.

De Bruyckere, P., P.A. Kirschner, and C. Hulshof. 2015. *Urban Myths About Learning and Education.* London: Academic Press.

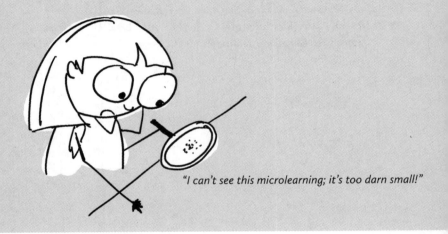

"I can't see this microlearning; it's too darn small!"

MICROLEARNING

THE CLAIM

Microlearning, small bits of content,
is the solution to learning.

Many organizations are promising that microlearning is a better approach. They claim that breaking information into small chunks actually better aligns with how our brains work. And chunking information makes learners happier, too. As evidence, proponents cite the numbers of people turning to YouTube videos to learn how to cook a recipe, change a tire, or be a better leader. They see the desire for short video content. And they believe that if we dribble these little bits out over time, people will learn more effectively and put up less resistance.

Another supportive argument is that these microlearning chunks are easy to create, and they allow learners to access them as they want or on a schedule.

THE COUNTER

Microlearning has become an umbrella term to encompass several different facets of learning. They include performance support, spaced learning, and contextualized learning. If you don't understand these facets separately and put them together in a way that promotes learning, you're really not going to get an effective program. What you'll get instead is a bill and a lot of feel-good anecdotes about being hip and current.

The just-in-time videos are often used as performance support, not to train. And that's okay, because they can help workers get the job done. But by terming it microlearning, people can delude themselves that they're also developing the workforce over time. While that's possible, it's not likely.

To actually create learning, you need a couple other things in addition to your short videos. Too often, what's proposed is to take a big course, break it down into small chunks, and stream them out. That sounds good, but it's missing the nuances of learning. It takes repeated practice, over time, interleaved with other retrieval, and revisited. And very few learning designers who adopt microlearning principles are actually addressing these details.

Instead, microlearning is being portrayed as a panacea, and that's a garden path to expenses that aren't matched by outcomes.

RECONCILIATION

The fact is, streaming small chunks over time is how we learn. However, before we can create effective microlearning, we need to understand when people need to learn and how best to deliver it. That takes more instructional design to figure out what bits, what repetition, how to interleave, and so on.

Another reconciliation is that if you use microlearning chunks to perform a task effectively and efficiently, it's okay if you aren't learning in the traditional sense. In fact, you should use performance support when you can! Too often, we think knowledge has to (at least eventually) be in the head. But that's not true. It's actually preferable for information to be in the world (that is, knowledge in the form of tables, checklists, and so forth that you can look up). It's hard to reliably get information into the head, because our brains aren't good at rote memory and recitation. This is especially true if the information is volatile (changing frequently) or unique enough that it's not worth trying to get everyone to know it.

WHAT TO DO

There's great value in having a platform that can support both the push and pull of short useful chunks of learning content. If we provide searchable indexes from which workers can pull pieces to show them how to do something, it could replace training! *And* still get the job done.

If you're invested in developing people, you can (and arguably should) still use small chunks, but you need a serious curricula design. An appropriate design understands how long the knowledge or skill is likely to persist, and reinforces again and again until you expect it's been fully internalized. In between, it should also continue to push out new content.

So, microlearning can be good, but know which aspect you're aiming for, and design appropriately. Don't assume.

CITATION

Quinn, C. 2017. "Microlearning Under the Microscope." Litmos Blog, May 23. www.litmos.com/blog/learning/microlearning-under-the-microscope.

PROBLEM-BASED LEARNING

THE CLAIM

Problem-based learning naturally integrates interest and leads to better outcomes.

Problem-based learning—which in some sense is an umbrella term for constructivist approaches where the learner discovers understanding through active experimentation—has been lauded as a more engaging and effective form of learning.

The typical approach, presenting learners with problems and providing resources for their solution, is seen as a more natural way to learn. Considerations include careful choices of those problems and resources, and providing scaffolding (gradually faded) for performance. Alternatively, learners can choose what they're interested in, and the instructor facilitates learning around the topic.

First, the use of meaningful problems instead of arbitrary problems is preferable because it maintains learner interest. In addition, the notion is that by using meaningful problems, instead of the abstract problems often used in direct instruction, learners will gain a richer understanding of the content.

This process is also called discovery learning, because the learners try a variety of approaches as they actively work to solve the problem. There's an expectation that by doing so, the learning is more persistent.

Educational reformer David H. Jonassen investigated problem-solving instruction for years. He found that while learners taught with problem-based approaches didn't perform as well on immediate tests, they retained the information better and transferred it to more appropriate problems. This suggests that problem-based approaches have the most valuable outcomes if you take the long-term view.

THE COUNTER

There is a strong view that direct instruction—presented concepts, examples, and practice activities—is the proven path for the most effective learning. Decades of research starting with the behaviorist tradition, including mastery learning, has provided empirical results that let us know which approaches optimize learning outcomes.

Educational researchers Paul A. Kirschner, John Sweller, and Richard E. Clark (2006) argued that direct instruction was superior to discovery learning and is the fastest path to achieve learning outcomes. Characterizing the opposition, they pointed to evidence showing the superiority of traditional learning methods.

RECONCILIATION

I've heard Clark speak, have met and talked with Sweller and the late Jonassen, and communicated with Kirschner. I respect all the participants (and would be loath to offend them); so I've no particular reason to distrust either side. Each has a sustained record of contribution to the field, so it's not easy to decide whether one approach is stronger than the other. Instead, we need to find a useful way to move forward.

There are a wide range of approaches that fall under the problem-based learning umbrella, including case studies and constructivism. As such, we need to be specific about what we're calling problem-based learning. While I like social constructivism, social learning is a topic for a separate treatment. Here I want to focus on providing learners with meaningful problems and scaffolding their investigations.

To be clear, I'm not talking about pure discovery. While that could be viewed as a possible approach, psychologist Reuven Feuerstein was discussing "guided" discovery around 1985. It's known that learners can prematurely limit their explorations, minimizing the benefits of an exploratory environment. Facilitation is also known to be a necessary adjunct to optimizing outcomes, as well as helping develop learning-to-learn skills.

There are two concomitant requirements to successful problem-based learning: carefully designed problems and skilled facilitators. Both present challenges. Finding the intersection between problems that draw upon the necessary skills and are also of intrinsic interest to participants is nontrivial. And by no means are even trained instructors capable of the specific role of learning facilitator without preparation.

The most compelling argument I've found so far is a paper by Johannes Strobel and Angela van Barneveld (2009). Performing a meta-analysis on problem-based learning, they determined that indeed, performance wasn't necessarily better on formal assessment, but it did lead to better retention and transfer (our learning goals). This resonates with Jonassen's findings, and is, to me, the key. Direct instruction definitely trumps poorly designed or pure discovery learning, but well-designed problem-based learning is optimal. I admit I'm more concerned about long-term performance than immediate assessment. (Unfortunately this is largely contrary to many forms of training and education, which evaluate only the immediately subsequent performance of an initiative.)

WHAT TO DO

Providing resources such as models and examples does facilitate learning. So, too, do intrinsic motivation and challenge. The reconciliation to me is a problem-based pedagogy that foregrounds meaningful problems, provides resources for success, and facilitates the process.

In the absence of facilitation with a problem-based approach, it may well be that direct instruction is the best design. Regardless of the approach, we need rigor around:

- practice items that require retrieval and application of knowledge in meaningful contexts
- concept presentations that include rich models to guide performance
- examples that illustrate the application of the concept to specific contexts, annotated with the underlying thinking
- tapping into intrinsic interest to drive engagement with the process and outcome.

The pedagogy around this may be concept first or problem first, it simply depends on the skill or availability of facilitators.

CITATIONS

Jonassen, D.H., J. Howland, J. Moore, and R.M. Marra. 2003. *Learning to Solve Problems With Technology: A Constructivist Perspective*, 2nd. Ed. Columbus, OH: Merrill/Prentice-Hall.

Kirschner, P.A., J. Sweller, and R.E. Clark. 2006. "Why Minimal Guidance During Instruction Does Not Work: An Analysis of the Failure of Constructivist, Discovery, Problem-Based, Experiential, and Inquiry-Based Teaching." *Educational Psychologist* 41(2): 75-86.

Strobel, J., and A. van Barneveld. 2009. "When is PBL More Effective? A Meta-Synthesis of Meta-Analyses Comparing PBL to Conventional Classrooms." *Interdisciplinary Journal of Problem-Based Learning* 3(1): 44-58.

"I told her I liked her, but she said my tone and body language said differently!"

7-38-55

THE CLAIM

Communication is 7 percent words, 38 percent tone, and 55 percent body language.

As taught in many communication and business courses, the message you communicate is interpreted based on 7 percent of what you say, 38 percent of how you say it, and 55 percent of how your face is composed while saying it. This number ratio is the result of research by psychologist Albert Mehrabian, who spent decades studying the effect of verbal and nonverbal messages. The clear implication is that we have to ensure a clear alignment between what we say and how we say it. Our communication approaches must be richer.

THE COUNTER

Despite some intuitive appeal, this claim just can't be right. Yes, we process more than the words, but should we only use phone calls so we're not countering our message with our facial expressions? Despite some challenges, technology-mediated conversations aren't less than half as effective. This doesn't pass the practicality test.

RECONCILIATION

Despite its prevalence in communication courses, even Mehrabian said that there were very strict limits on how far to extend his findings. For one, his research specifically examined how we communicate feelings and attitudes, not general communication! Second, this ratio was intended only for situations where no other information about the relationship was available. That's a very limited set of all our communications.

WHAT TO DO

First, don't propagate this message without clarification, and challenge those who do! Second, be careful with your tone and body language when communicating, but also make sure the message is appropriate and authentic. The full picture of communication includes what you say and how you say it, but also what prior knowledge listeners bring to the situation. Don't follow simplistic equations, but do be aware.

CITATION

Mehrabian, A. 1971. *Silent Messages,* 1st ed. Belmont, CA: Wadsworth.

"Hey, we're doing Level 1. It's a start."

KIRKPATRICK MODEL OF EVALUATION

THE CLAIM

The Kirkpatrick model isn't an effective evaluation model.

Many learning professionals, including some of my friends and colleagues, deride the Kirkpatrick model. They say it reinforces training, but doesn't measure learning. Further, they accuse it of making it easy for folks to settle for smile sheets. In general, it is viewed as a dinosaur.

The Kirkpatrick model, if you've somehow missed hearing or reading about it, is a four-stage model for evaluating the effectiveness of performance initiatives. Developed by Don Kirkpatrick in the 1950s, and the basis of his and his son's subsequent careers, the model postulates the following levels:

- **Level 1: Reaction.** Did participants find the training favorable, engaging, and relevant to their jobs?
- **Level 2: Learning.** Did participants acquire the intended knowledge, skills, attitude, confidence, and commitment based on their participation in the training?
- **Level 3: Behavior.** Did participants apply what they learned during training when they were back on the job?
- **Level 4: Results.** Which targeted outcomes occurred as a result of the training and the support and accountability package?

The biggest claim against the Kirkpatrick model is that it is specifically focused on training, and makes it easy to just do Level 1 evaluation and feel like you are doing something meaningful.

It is well documented that most organizations stop at Level 1, occasionally Level 2. Further, the subjective evaluation of the effectiveness of learning has little correlation with the actual effectiveness of the outcome. As seen in the learning superstition Smile Sheets = Evaluation, this isn't a useful indicator.

It's argued that if the goal is to determine whether people gained a new ability due to the training, Kirkpatrick doesn't solve the problem. People instead suggest Brinkerhoff's method, Daniel Stufflebeam's CIPP (context, input, process, product) model, or other evaluation models.

THE COUNTER

The Kirkpatricks and their adherents characterize the model not as an evaluation of the learning (or training), but rather as a way to evaluate the effectiveness of the training for the organization. That is, is the training having a business impact? That's the question they believe is important to document.

They believe that it is wrong to just do Level 1 or even Level 2, and that you're supposed to start with Level 4. (I even heard Don himself admit he probably numbered it wrong.) If you're not starting with Level 4, you're not following the model. James and Wendy Kirkpatrick argue as much in their 2016 update, *Kirkpatrick's Four Levels of Evaluation*. Any problems then are with the implementation, not the model.

The goal is to start with the organizational need and work backward. You should identify a gap in performance and figure out what change in behavior will improve the situation. Then, you design training to achieve that change, evaluate whether the training is working, assess whether the behavior has changed, and finally determine if the business need is addressed.

RECONCILIATION

It is clear that the role the Kirkpatrick model plays in L&D is muddied. Indeed, it has been used to justify simplistic and ineffective evaluation. Yes, it's not a learning evaluation approach, and the Kirkpatricks do overemphasize training. Level 1 is at best a luxury, and might even be unnecessary. But, to me, the bottom line is that it's useful.

Starting with Level 4 is the correct approach. That's what performance consulting is about. And, if the initiative is a job aid or a change in incentives, you can still use Kirkpatrick to evaluate it. It works beyond training. When you use the model correctly, it focuses attention at the right spot.

Most importantly, there's little else that points in that direction. In my mind, Kirkpatrick is a design tool. Starting with Level 4 makes it obvious that you want to improve business outcomes. Working backward from there is a valuable approach!

So I've tackled the misconception around Kirkpatrick somewhat differently. I argue that Kirkpatrick is a useful framework to think about needed performance initiatives and assess whether they're working. You can use tools like Brinkerhoff and others within Level 2 to evaluate whether the training is effective. You can use approaches like manager reviews, instrumented applications, or customer evaluations to see if Level 3 is being addressed. Business metrics are the ultimate evaluation of Level 4. And this is a good thing, to the extent that it keeps me from wanting to overthrow Kirkpatrick.

(Disclosure: I have a contribution in one chapter of the cited work. I did so for the arguments here, and there are no financial returns.)

WHAT TO DO

Use any approach you want—performance consulting, Kirkpatrick, whatever—but do start with the business need. When it comes to evaluating whether your learning, training, or performance initiative is working, use something appropriate. But then, work back up and see if it's actually leading to the intended behavior change and business impact. Will Thalheimer has just released his L-TEM model, and it looks to be a better basis with the same strengths but greater detail.

CITATION

Kirkpatrick, J.D., and W.K. Kirkpatrick. 2016. *Kirkpatrick's Four Levels of Training Evaluation.* Alexandria, VA: ATD Press.

NeuroX or BrainX

THE CLAIM

NeuroX or BrainX (where X = learning, leadership, and so on) has important lessons.

You've probably seen it: NeuroLearning or NeuroLeadership or similar. This is also known under the term brain-based. The story is that research in neuroscience has provided valuable new insights, which range from the relatively sober to such extreme views as "human learning is about to change forever!"

Brain science is advancing. With tools like Magnetic Resonance Imaging (MRI), our understanding of the brain has expanded rapidly. It makes sense that we should track the implications for learning and work.

THE COUNTER

Despite the advances at the level of neural understanding, most of the implications are better understood at a cognitive level, not a neural level, as psychologist Daniel Willingham tells us. We already knew that learning involves strengthening the connections between patterns in the brain, but the ways we do that are addressed at higher levels.

Touting results as "neural" can be appropriate when the results are at that level, but while that level of operation plays a role, the manifestations and, more importantly, the mechanisms to influence workplace learning practices are almost completely at the cognitive and higher levels.

Moreover, cognitive science as a term was deliberately chosen as a way to integrate findings from disparate fields that affect our thinking. These findings range from neuroscience to social learning, and include anthropology, sociology, philosophy, education, linguistics, and psychology.

RECONCILIATION

Unfortunately, companies and their representatives are using *neural* and *brain-based* as a marketing tactic for their "new" approaches; a shiny new object, if you will. Whether it's using neuroscience to justify approaches already known from learning science or, worse, taking data inappropriately out of context, it's not an accurate inference.

Yes, we're finding out that the neurotransmitter dopamine plays a role in motivation, but that just means that we should create intrinsic interest in our content. Understanding the mechanism doesn't necessarily provide a good basis for determining the useful implications, but it does generate attention-getting copy!

We do want to understand the mechanisms and their implications, but we have to do it holistically. We need to separate out the hype from the practicalities. Hype sells, but practicalities lead to real change. And as practitioners, we should care for the latter.

WHAT TO DO

To be an aware consumer, we need to have a basic understanding of our brains and how we learn. That's important for designing learning as a professional as well as a basis for interpreting new claims. There's a brief overview in this book's introductory chapters.

Second, we must be discriminating consumers. If we fall for hype, we will certainly be subject to more. We have to ask for the ultimate implications, and see if they're truly different from good practices we already know.

CITATION

Willingham, D.T. 2009. "Three Problems in the Marriage of Neuroscience and Education." *Cortex* 45(4): 544-545.

"If you learned it through others, it doesn't count."

SOCIAL LEARNING

THE CLAIM

Social learning is all hype.

A number of people, learning experts and corporate executives alike, have stipulated that social learning is a waste of resources. They consider the desired performance to be the end state, and all that's required to achieve it is a sequence of activities with feedback to support the learner.

When we're training for a specific performance, we can create an environment that is wired for feedback, where we have very specific tasks. People can explore, discover relationships, and get feedback to shape their understanding. If we get past the trivial response that all learning is social (because whoever created the resources and experience were people), we have examples where people acquire the necessary knowledge without involving others.

THE COUNTER

The strong argument for social learning comes from the fact that if an individual processes something, there's no guarantee that the interpretation they receive is sufficient. And to effectively address that takes either interaction with other learners or an expert. Thus, social learning can have significant benefits.

The cognitive story is fairly simple. When we're taught material, we create only one interpretation of that information. However, if we interact with others and hear their interpretations, we'll see different ways of viewing the topic. Having multiple viewpoints is especially important when we're engaged in an activity that requires us to provide a unified output, because we have to negotiate a shared understanding with others. And that enhanced knowledge negotiation enriches each individual's understanding.

If you've ever taught, you've probably had a student come up with an interpretation that you'd never believed possible. And there's value in that, if the new interpretation can be seen and shared. The instructional role is to facilitate the exchange of viewpoints and ensure negotiation of a shared understanding.

In addition, when the varied interpretations emerge through social engagement between learners, it can short-circuit the necessity of trying to

cover all those perspectives. While we can't guarantee that knowledge negotiation will erase all misconceptions, it's likely to produce a richer understanding than a sole perusal of the materials.

RECONCILIATION

The real issue is figuring out when social learning makes sense, rather
than having an either/or position. We get a richer understanding when we
have people exchange viewpoints. But that can take more time. When does
setting aside this extra time make sense?

The determinants are the complexity of the material and how far the
transfer is across contexts. If your goal is to get the mind around complex
interplays, then it makes sense to include more social interaction around
the material. If instead you're training people to do one very specific task or
letting learners pursue their own learning, social learning becomes less beneficial. (Side note: I think more and more of the latter example of jobs—those
that are rote execution—will be automated, so the need for social learning
will be more likely.) Social is a critical component of informal learning, but it
should be facilitated, not enforced.

WHAT TO DO

Look for opportunities to engage peers and mentors into the learning
experience. For asynchronous e-learning, solo is the typical way to go.
But individuals may well benefit from seeing what others have thought,
so having a way to capture and share the generated ideas and interpretations is valuable. When we're in the classroom, we should use the time for
meaningful engagement, not content delivery (think: blended learning).
And we can use discussion boards and collaborative documents in the
online classroom. Incorporating group projects into our designs is also a
useful idea.

We should also think about extending the learning experience with
coaching. Having people engaged after the "event" (and hopefully you're
thinking "experience" instead) on an ongoing, though tapering, basis is the
key to solidifying the knowledge.

Finally, don't assume that your learners have social learning skills. They're typically not taught, but there are good models. Develop them as part of formal learning.

CITATION

Quinn, C. 2009. "Social Networking: Bridging Formal and Informal Learning." Learning Solutions, February 23. www.learningsolutionsmag.com /articles/57/social-networking-bridging-formal-and-informal-learning.

"I couldn't help it, it just unlearned itself."

UNLEARNING

THE CLAIM

The key skill in an era of increasing change is the ability to unlearn.

As things change, much of what we've taken for granted has been shown to be wrong. Whether the question is "Is fat or sugar a bigger problem?" or "Should ice be used for injuries?" there's a constant churn in beliefs. Consequently, the notion that we may have to unlearn things has gained traction, and unlearning is touted as the new skill.

Future Shock author Alvin Toffler wrote:

> "The illiterate of the 21st century will not be those who cannot read and write, but those who cannot learn, unlearn, and relearn."

This viewpoint suggests that unlearning is a "thing." The open question is whether unlearning itself can be learned.

THE COUNTER

As a contrary viewpoint, the psychological consensus is that we don't forget (or unlearn) things, they just get increasingly harder to trigger or retrieve. And researchers John Howells and Joachim Scholderer's review of the use of the term in organizational learning found no evidence for the term itself. Most people have had the phenomenon of a scent or sound or sighting triggering a long-lost memory. Can we really unlearn this involuntary reaction?

The cognitive science story of strengthening associations between neurons doesn't have a counterapproach for weakening connections. There's no known mechanism for this occurring.

RECONCILIATION

What unlearning really consists of is "overlearning"; that is, training new reactions until they're stronger than the old patterns, and more likely to occur when called on. Basically, we learn "over" the old traces. This may take considerable practice, so the ideal is to learn only things that are not likely to change, and put more volatile information in the world where it is easily referenced and can be subject to change without disrupting the overall performance.

WHAT TO DO

It's okay to use the term *unlearning* as long as it doesn't lead to misconceptions about how to address preexisting knowledge that needs to be changed. When you do need to learn something new, care has to be taken to prevent falling into bad habits. Scaffolding such as checklists or coaching can help.

From a design perspective, a good principle is to avoid asking people to learn things that may change. Things that can change should be accessed and used without being remembered, so what's retained is the process of finding the information, not the information itself.

CITATIONS

Howells, J., and J. Scholderer. 2016. "Forget Unlearning? How an Empirically Unwarranted Concept From Psychology Was Imported to Flourish in Management and Organization Studies." *Management Learning* 47:4.

Toffler, A. 1970. *Future Shock.* New York: Random House.

BRAINSTORMING

THE CLAIM

Brainstorming doesn't work.

Several recent articles have claimed that brainstorming doesn't work. The original concept of brainstorming suggests that people get together, consider a problem, offer their ideas, and work through them. This approach was countered with evidence that group idea generation yields fewer ideas than when individuals work alone to produce ideas. Thus, they claim, the original approach is flawed.

Their ultimate problem with brainstorming comes down to "groupthink." When people are brainstorming in the traditional sense, the first person who says something constrains other people's thinking. As a result, these brainstorming denouncers tend to posit other approaches. Whether it's writing, splitting up, or bodystorming (a form of brainstorming in which you use experiences to derive new ideas), the idea is to avoid the groupthink problem.

THE COUNTER

Pulling people together to solve problems is reliably superior to going at them alone. We know that combining a variety of backgrounds and experiences leads to a better output. We need to find a way to tap into the power of diversity without finding a constraint.

RECONCILIATION

In his overview of brainstorming research, investigator Scott G. Isaksen (1998) joined in the claim that brainstorming may be "the most researched and least understood creative thinking technique"! When brainstorming, it is important to iterate between thinking as an individual and as a group—you want everyone to generate their own thoughts, and then you want to bring them together. There's power in individual variety, and there's power in the group seeing what others have come up with and letting the lateral inputs spark new ideas.

Other activities also foster creativity, like allowing time for ideas to percolate. So think about bringing people back the next day for further discussion (have them write down ideas when they wake up, thus taking advantage of sleep). Another option is to combine the process with nature, as the surroundings tend to foster mindstates more conducive to reflective thought.

The approach you end up using may not qualify as the original brainstorming process. That's OK. What you want is a process that creates results; one that ensures everyone ideates individually, and everyone gets a voice.

WHAT TO DO

First, you need to have everyone think on their own about the problem and generate ideas to solve it. This can happen either before everyone gets together or at the beginning of a meeting. Then, when everyone's generated a breadth of ideas, bring them together and have a discussion process. It's important to let everyone have a chance to speak, to ensure ideas aren't lost. It's also necessary to make the environment feel safe (even fun) to share ideas. The process must be managed to make it comfortable to participate and be different. This process can be cycled, returning to individual and then group think. Feel free to spread it out, over time or across geography.

CITATION

Isaksen, S.G. 1998. *A Review of Brainstorming Research: Six Critical Issues for Inquiry.* Buffalo, NY: Creative Problem Solving Group.

"I'm sorry, but you didn't close the sale. I'm afraid you're fired."

"But I had the highest score on the quizzes!"

GAMIFICATION

THE CLAIM

Gamification is a valuable contribution to achieving learning outcomes.

Gamification has definitely hit the big time. It's now being built in to most learning management systems, and many authoring tools for learning content let you add competition themes to your quizzes. In short, it's the missing ingredient to make learning engaging.

Gamification has many facets, but one popular notion is the "PBL" approach: points, badges, and leaderboards. Other more-nuanced approaches talk about adding gameplay mechanisms to e-learning, allowing you to leverage the tricks that make computer games addictive.

In short, with gamification, you can take dull, dreary training, and motivate your learners to want to stay involved.

THE COUNTER

Some gamification experts have opined that indiscriminately adding points and other such competition components can have a detrimental effect on learning. There's also a concern that over time, the appeal of gamification will wear off, and learners will fall back into traditional patterns of avoidance and apathy toward training.

Others look to make a distinction between intrinsic and extrinsic motivation, putting the PBL elements very much on the side of extrinsic motivation. They point out that intrinsic motivation, whereby learners find the material and challenges inherently interesting, is a more powerful and persistent outcome.

The distinction they want to make is the need to tap into serious games as intrinsic motivation, and leave off the gratuitous extras. The belief is that finding the intrinsic interest in the training program will motivate effort and support learning, which is a better holistic outcome.

RECONCILIATION

Researcher Karl Kapp has made the distinction between gamification and serious games, and that distinction is important. Generating intrinsic interest is better, but it's also harder to achieve. It takes special knowledge and skills to systematically make learning meaningful to both the learner and the domain. While it's possible, it can take somewhat longer until those skills are developed.

However, that doesn't mean we shouldn't make the effort. As mentioned, there are learning and learner benefits from intrinsic interest. One way to do so is to make the questions meaningful, so that they're mini-scenarios instead of just a knowledge exam.

And there are quantitative benefits to gamification, too. People can be motivated by scores, and badges that acknowledge increasing capability are a common feature. Recognition of effort is intrinsic as well.

WHAT TO DO

The best approach is to focus on finding the intrinsic interest. Subject matter experts are great resources—they've clearly found the field interesting enough to become experts at it. Tap into their fascination, and bake it into the learning. Learners appreciate enthusiasm.

Note that this is true even for compliance training. Training often becomes a knowledge-dump because it's easy, but that won't lead to any better outcomes. The effort to find the intrinsic interest is valuable regardless of topic. Make it meaningful, and make it useful!

Then, use gamification as an adjunct after you find the intrinsic interest. There's nothing wrong with trying to enhance the engagement. Just be careful to avoid rewarding the wrong behaviors. That's the risk.

CITATION

Kapp, K. 2012. *The Gamification of Learning and Instruction: Game-Based Methods and Strategies for Training and Education.* Alexandria, VA: ASTD Press.

"I only meta-learn!"

"Um, then do you learn anything at all?"

META-LEARNING

THE CLAIM

There are no domain-independent learning skills.

Meta-learning, or learning to learn, has been widely touted as the only sustainable approach for a future in which the half-life of information is less than the time spent earning a college degree.

However, I have heard notable cognitive scientists suggest that there are no real domain-independent learning skills; instead, problem-solving skills are very much tied to specific areas. For example, there are skills required for mathematics, but each branch of engineering has other skills, and so on. The absence of general skills suggests that you need expertise in your domains of practice, as well as the associated learning skills in that domain. You need to understand what constitutes acceptable knowledge, respected practice, and more in that field.

Research by the National Research Council (2000) suggests novices differ from experts in that their initial searches don't benefit from the complex knowledge and pattern matching that allows experts to proceed faster. Local domain knowledge can be taught, but otherwise, acquisition is slow, idiosyncratic, and likely to be localized.

THE COUNTER

Several strategies for meta-learning have proved to be effective. A 2013 investigation by psychologist John Dunlosky and others showed that using practice testing and spaced practice could help develop skills. Such strategies as self-explanation, interleaved practice, and elaborative interrogation also had their use. Surprisingly, Dunlosky found that highlighting and underlining, summarization, and rereading were unlikely to lead to any better learning outcomes, which is contrary to many beliefs. Other research, summarized by Françoise Boch and Annie Piolat, has shown note taking to be a complex practice, and it's effectiveness greatly depends on the style and further use of the notes.

Similarly, psychologist Carol Dweck's research on the growth mindset (whereby people believe that their intelligence can get better, versus a fixed mindset) shows that the learner's beliefs and consequential performance can be improved. Rather than persisting with beliefs about an unchangeable level of intelligence, beliefs in the malleability of intelligence can lead to better performance.

Note also the research on digital natives summarized elsewhere in this tome, and recognize that not just literacy but digital literacy skills are needed and can't be assumed. Such skills are likely to underpin success in research across domains and, consequently, on learning.

RECONCILIATION

While meta-learning effects may be weaker than domain-specific skills, the application may be far broader. As domains are undergoing rapid change, it is increasingly likely that learning to learn will be the sole differentiator. While there will definitely be domain-specific strategies, domain-independent strategies appear to be trainable and valuable as well. Neglecting either would be less than optimal.

WHAT TO DO

Increasingly, it will make sense to consider meta-learning skills. Given that the education system is idiosyncratic (diplomatically speaking) about developing these skills, it behooves organizations to identify valuable skills, assess them, and develop them. Leaving the skills to chance will be an impediment to organizational success. Skills likely to be worth looking at will also include working together, such as collaborative problem solving, and research skills.

CITATIONS

Blackwell, L.S., K.H. Trzesniewski, and C.S. Dweck. 2007. "Implicit Theories of Intelligence Predict Achievement Across an Adolescent Transition: A Longitudinal Study and an Intervention." *Child Development* 78:1.

Boch, F., and A. Piolat. 2005. "Note Taking and Learning: A Summary of Research." *The WAC Journal*, 16.

Dunlosky, J., K.A. Rawson, E.J. Marsh, M.J. Nathan, and D.T. Willingham. 2013. "Improving Students' Learning With Effective Learning Techniques: Promising Directions from Cognitive and Educational Psychology." *Psychological Science in the Public Interest* 14:1.

National Research Council. 2000. *How People Learn: Brain, Mind, Experience, and School: Expanded Edition.* Washington, D.C.: The National Academies Press.

HUMOR IN LEARNING

THE CLAIM

Avoid using humor in learning.

Some learning experts and educators believe that humor should be avoided in training for principled reasons—it detracts from the seriousness of the topic. Others feel it should be avoided for pragmatic reasons—it is hard to do humor well. Individually, these claims seem sufficient to proscribe the use of humor, and together, they make a pretty good case.

There's certainly evidence that humor can be hard to do reliably. For evidence, you need only look at the failed situation TV comedies, unfunny movies, theatre, and other media. Obviously, someone thought they were funny, because they were produced, but their failure shows that what one considers humorous isn't always predictable. Not to mention the evidence that humor often fails to transcend the boundaries of culture.

THE COUNTER

On the other hand, a light mood can facilitate learning, particularly at the start of whatever learning experience you're designing. Exploring broadly in pursuit of learning is facilitated by a positive atmosphere; later, when depth is needed, a harsher environment can drive people to limit their exploration and work harder. Others, myself included, have suggested that learning can and should be "hard fun."

Evidence also suggests that humor can build community, and that it boosts dopamine levels (as does achieving learning goals).

RECONCILIATION

Not surprisingly, the compromise is all about when and how to use humor. Humor is neither good nor bad—it's good when used appropriately and bad when used inappropriately. A meta-analysis of 40 years of humor research by John A. Banas and colleagues provides us with some solid recommendations. For example, it's bad practice to use humor at the expense of your learners, on inappropriate topics, and too frequently.

WHAT TO DO

The recommendations are not complete, but they are indicative. Jana Hackathorn and colleagues found that humor increases learning outcomes, at least for retaining knowledge. For one, instructors (and, presumably, designers) should use material that reflects their own personality or style. Humor should also be positive and inclusive. Use humor to make points relevant to the lesson—for example, humor about business itself and the characteristics of business are likely to be relevant in most organizational settings and, consequently, organizational learning.

CITATIONS

Banas, J.A., N. Dunbar, D. Rodriguez, and S. Liu. 2011. "A Review of Humor in Education Settings: Four Decades of Research." *Communication Education* 60:1.

Hackathorn, J., A.M. Garczynski, K. Blankmeyer, R.D. Tennial, and E.D. Solomon. 2011. "All Kidding Aside: Humor Increases Learning at Knowledge and Comprehension Levels." *Journal of the Scholarship of Teaching and Learning* 11:4.

"I learned all this on my phone!"

MLEARNING

THE CLAIM

Any learning through a mobile device is mLearning.

For many, mobile learning (or mLearning) is about learning through a mobile device, period. That's what the name implies, after all. This means presenting a full course on the device, or providing access to information that people need in the moment to answer their questions and let them learn (note that this isn't information to help them *do* something, just information *about* things). Anything more just, well, isn't mobile learning.

THE COUNTER

If you're concerned only with learning, you're not looking at the full picture of supporting people to be successful. Most of us don't learn for intellectual self-gratification; we learn to be able to do something new. With that perspective, we can view mobile learning in a much broader scope.

Mobile learning can be used to support performance, connect to colleagues to get things done, and do things because of when and where we are. If you think mLearning is just about courses on a phone, you're missing a whole suite of opportunities.

RECONCILIATION

These perspectives don't have to be in conflict; mLearning can mean learning through a device and doing other things to support people both performing in the moment and developing over time. My exploration into mobile made it clear that there is much more possible, and I've subsequently recommended that learning and development could, and should, be looking at performance support as well as social and informal learning. This is all part of a more strategic stance for talent development.

WHAT TO DO

Consider the full repertoire of ways mobile devices can support people being more effective in the moment and over time. Mobile is a platform—a way to reach people when and where they are with solutions to the full suite of needs.

CITATIONS

Quinn, C.N. 2011. *Designing mLearning: Tapping Into the Mobile Revolution for Organizational Performance.* Pfeiffer: San Francisco.

——— 2014. *Revolutionize Learning & Development: Performance and Innovation Strategy for the Information Age.* San Francisco: Wiley.

THE EXPERIENCE API

THE CLAIM

xAPI is an important step beyond
course tracking.

The Experience API (xAPI) was developed as a successor to SCORM (the Sharable Content Object Reference Model) as a way to collect data on learners, extending past the SCORM model of reporting on course start and completion. The demand stemmed from a need to investigate other resources beyond courses. Inspired by activity-tracking on the web, the Advanced Distributed Learning project of the Department of Defense developed xAPI (which was briefly known as TinCan).

xAPI provides a simple syntax that records who – did – what. That is, you can say, "Pat read *Revolutionize L&D*" or "Chris accessed JobAid 14." It can also say, "Dale completed ComplianceCourse1132." What this provides is a simple mechanism for recording activity. And, more importantly, it's a standard one.

THE COUNTER

However, those data alone are of no use. What does it matter who did what? Unless they're coupled with other data, the actions people take aren't going to be useful in determining individual ability or organization development.

Another complaint is that many actions that characterize informal learning—ways in which people meet their learning needs—aren't trackable by xAPI. If we can't track relevant material, what we have is irrelevant.

Moreover, to do anything useful with those data, you need additional resources. For one, it's been recognized that xAPI struggles to do what SCORM did; CMI 5 is an approach to try to add an additional layer of data description to make xAPI useful for courses. The data also need to be housed, so a learning record system (LRS) is the usual requirement to use xAPI.

Most importantly, there's now a competing standard. The IMS Project, a product of Educause, released Caliper as a standard that is very similar to xAPI. The benefits of standards are undermined when such standards compete.

RECONCILIATION

It's true that xAPI isn't sufficient by itself. However, what it does add is important, as practitioner Sean Putnam and colleagues have argued. Having a standard syntax means that it's possible to build reporting that leverages a standard. And, the benefits of standards are that they open up innovation. In addition, IMS and the ADL have started working toward a reconciliation between Caliper and xAPI.

More importantly, while xAPI by itself isn't obviously of use, it provides a standard basis for using such data with business intelligence to get those important answers. Correlations between meaningful business data, such as errors, customer ratings, or sales, can be looked at in conjunction with employee actions to start determining which actions are of use and which aren't. Beyond looking at the questions you want answered, you can also use data mining to explore new outcomes.

While not all data can be collected, much can be automatically generated by instrumenting relevant systems. Portals and social media can generate activity information that, by itself, may not be useful, but can provide insight when collated with outcomes. You can also ask people to report. You'll have to address some issues in design to make it easy and in policy and culture to make it consistent, but it is possible.

This is the era of big data and analytics. Increasingly, we should be looking at measurement as a tool to investigate what is and should be happening. xAPI is a useful tool to accomplish that goal.

WHAT TO DO

Get on top of xAPI, and start thinking about using data as a critical element in determining what to do, how it's going, and what needs to be changed. You'll want to start thinking about what you should measure (including not just efficiency about courses offered, but effectiveness in terms of impact). Also, start thinking about what you can measure. Measurement is part of strategy, and it's past time for talent development to get strategic.

CITATION

Putnam, S., J.L. Effron, and M. Bowe. 2017. *Investigating Performance: Design & Outcomes With xAPI*. Pennsauken, NJ: Bookbaby.

"Successfully making a sale is on Bloom's?"

BLOOM'S TAXONOMY

THE CLAIM

Bloom's Taxonomy is a useful guide
for designing learning.

Ubiquitous in education and quite prevalent in corporate learning as well, Bloom's Taxonomy provides a structure for categorizing learning outcomes. Designers use this model to characterize learning outcomes at a specific level of cognitive complexity. Whether in its initial format or the revised version, the model proposes six levels of "knowing," with increasing complexity: remember, understand, apply, analyze, evaluate, create.

The goal of using Bloom's is to have a useful taxonomy for characterizing tasks. The belief is that it lets you build from lower-order tasks to higher-order, thus fostering thinking skills.

THE COUNTER

Brenda Sugrue has been the clearest voice in pointing out the problems with Bloom's Taxonomy and proposing alternatives that resonate with what learning science tells us. She makes clear that Bloom developed his initial taxonomy before cognitive science unpacked the different types of learning, and even the revised taxonomy doesn't align with what the latest research tells us.

Another complaint is that it is hard to reliably apply Bloom's Taxonomy. For example, designers can disagree about where a learning objective falls. The terms have too much overlap to be useful.

The final complaint is that the distinctions aren't useful. The first two levels are about knowing, while the three higher levels are about doing, which seems to be the important element anyway. The distinctions between the two categories aren't meaningful enough when it comes time to create learning.

RECONCILIATION

Taxonomies are useful to the extent that they help us understand what we should and shouldn't pay attention to. Consequently, having a useful categorization of learning components is helpful in design, but we need one that is both useful and robust.

Recent research has led to two major distinctions: the knowledge you need and the tasks you perform. Further research breaks the knowledge component down into four subcomponents: concept, fact, process, and principle.

WHAT TO DO

I suggest the approach Jeroen van Merriënboer has proposed: Focus on what learners need to do, and accompany that with the minimum information they need to be able to do it. Simplicity is more effective and efficient. What's the task they need to be able to do, or what decision do they need to be able to make? And what's the minimum information they need to be able to succeed?

CITATIONS

Sugrue, B. 2013. "A Learning Science Alternative to Bloom's Taxonomy." Learning Solutions, March 6. www.learningsolutionsmag.com /articles/1116/a-learning-science-alternative-to-blooms-taxonomy.

Van Merriënboer, J.J.G. 1997. *Training Complex Cognitive Skills: A Four-Component Instructional Design Model for Technical Training.* Englewood Cliffs, NJ: Educational Technology Publications.

LEARNING MANAGEMENT SYSTEMS

THE CLAIM

A learning management system is the key software to support learning and development.

When some learning professionals look at what L&D traditionally does, they see the learning management system (LMS) as the software that manages the core steps: hosting courses, scheduling events, supporting signups, tracking completions, and assuring compliance. The LMS allows us to track course access and completion, and align that with our resources so we can generate metrics on how efficient we are.

Moreover, newer LMSs also provide the capabilities that more modern approaches to L&D posit as important directions: social interaction, gamification for motivation, resources hosting and searching, video capability, and mobile access are on nearly every supplier's checklist of features. The LMS supports everything L&D needs to do.

THE COUNTER

Learning management is an oxymoron: You can't "manage" learning! These systems would be better called course management systems. And while managing courses is a plausible function, the whole notion of focusing on courses is antithetical to the new direction L&D is moving. We're not focused on courses, we're focused on optimizing performance and facilitating development.

As we understand more about learning, and start looking at the broader picture of what L&D could (and should) be doing, we see a different picture. A learning program needs to extend past the course to coaching and stretch assignments, for instance. And we need to consider other solutions to courses when we can, such as facilitating informal learning through communication and collaboration. We need to think beyond the course!

The LMS has courses in its DNA, and that means it's being patched to meld to the new model. Shouldn't we start fresh instead? Moreover, having one all-singing, all-dancing solution isn't optimal. To use the familiar metaphor: A Swiss Army knife is great when it's the only tool you have, but when you're in the kitchen you want a chef's knife and a cleaver and a paring knife—you want to use the right tool for the job. In the L&D space, you need a suite of software integrated into a coherent performance ecosystem.

RECONCILIATION

While courses aren't dead, there's a lot more to L&D than courses. Having a tool to manage courses makes sense, although it should be focused on managing learning experiences, including spacing the learning, coaching, and tracking related material that gets accessed over time.

Having one piece of software makes sense when you're too small to have the full suite, or when your IT group isn't capable of something broader. But increasingly, software is crossing silos and integrating with the organization; that's an approach L&D should be aligning with.

From an ecosystem perspective, the resources should be learner-centric: There should be portals to resources by role, with easily accessible communication and collaboration tools. Search should be federated, and individuals and groups should be able to find or create and share resources along with those created or curated by L&D. What we need is a different view of L&D, one that has supporting performance and development as the central focus, not courses.

WHAT TO DO

Start thinking about a performance ecosystem, not courses. Align your technology strategy to a performer-centric vision. An LMS may well be part of that ecosystem, but it's not the core. And be wary of anyone trying to sell you one piece of software that purports to "do it all."

CITATION

Quinn, C.N. 2014. *Revolutionize Learning & Development: Performance and Innovation Strategy for the Information Age.* San Francisco: Wiley.

CONCLUSION

Many beliefs can interfere with our ability to deliver learning experiences that benefit our learners and organizations. If we don't apply what's known, we can undermine our investments. Learning is a probabilistic game, and every misstep reduces the likelihood of successful application to the workplace. We become ineffective if we don't:

- Awaken relevant knowledge and emotionally engage learners.
- Provide rigorous practice.
- Create mental models to guide performance.
- Develop examples that illustrate the breadth of application from concept to context.

Unfortunately, professionalism in learning design has been lax in practice. The old canard, "Those who can't do, teach," seems to be in play. Too often folks who were good at their job or at stand-up training are thrust into the role of instructional designer with insufficient preparation. A knowledge of learning science is too infrequently seen.

Similarly, a belief that "if it looks like school, it must be learning" also seems to exist. Executives and managers are happy if there is content and a quiz. Yet information presentation followed by a knowledge test is very unlikely to lead to any new abilities.

Best Principles

We can't simply copy what others do. For all the talk about best practices, there's a fundamental flaw. Copying what worked in one context and thinking it will work the same in another demonstrates a limited understanding of the effect of the context. The reasons why things work are inextricably tied to the way things are operating in that particular situation. Changing the context without adapting the environment won't work, as many examples have demonstrated.

Instead, what's required is abstracting the principles underlying the success, and re-instantiating them in the new context. This is learning, but at the organizational level, not at the individual level. We want to learn how to apply these principles systematically.

So one approach could be to completely adopt a new approach: learn and implement a pre-existing approach. This would be considerably disruptive, and have some impediments to success, such as the status quo. Such efforts have a low likelihood of success without a comprehensive and informed change effort.

Another approach is to strategically determine which elements to introduce first, and how, and then gradually work to incorporate those elements before adding more. This may result in a slower process, but it has a greater likelihood for success. While the approach for any one organization will be unique, the best principles of organizational change still apply!

Caveat Emptor

The final take-home is the eternal admonition: "Buyer beware." An informed buyer is better equipped to avoid unfortunate expenses. My goal has been to provide an introduction to learning science and some skills for reviewing materials, as well as a resource to address many of the approaches you may be asked to consider.

This isn't a final, total solution. There are other suggestions that weren't incorporated because they were not considered central to organizational learning, yet they can pose challenges in many situations. And, just as science continues to advance, so too do proposals for new ways to achieve the outcomes you desire. You must, however, be cautious. Not every proposal will be legitimate, if past history is any indication. There always seem to be new folks who would like to separate you from your money, and aren't scrupulous about how scrutable they are!

I hope this work provides you a resource on a small investment that pays off in saving you from misspending a large amount. I wish you good—and smart—learning.

REFERENCES AND RESOURCES

Bransford, J.D., A.L. Brown, and R.R. Cocking. 2000. *How People Learn: Brain, Mind, Experience, and School.* Washington, D.C.: National Academies Press.

Brown, P.C., H.L. Roediger III, and M.A. McDaniel. 2014. *Make It Stick: The Science of Successful Learning.* Boston: Harvard University Press.

Carey, B. 2014. *How We Learn: The Surprising Truth About When, Where, and Why It Happens.* New York: Random House.

Clark, R.C., R.E. Mayer. 2011. *e-Learning and the Science of Instruction*, 3rd Edition. San Francisco: Pfeiffer.

Clark, R.C., F. Nguyen, and J. Sweller. 2006. *Efficiency in Learning: Evidence-Based Guidelines to Manage Cognitive Load.* San Francisco: Pfeiffer.

de Bruyckere, P., P.A. Kirschner, and C.D. Hulshof. 2015. *Urban Myths About Learning and Education.* Cambridge, MA: Academic Press.

Dirksen, J. 2015. *Design for How People Learn,* 2nd Edition. Berkeley, CA: New Riders Press.

Ericsson, A., and R. Pool. 2016. *Peak: Secrets From the New Science of Expertise.* Boston: Houghton Mifflin Harcourt.

Macdonald, K., L. Germine, A. Anderson, J. Christodoulou, and L.M. McGrath. 2017. "Dispelling the Myth: Training in Education or Neuroscience Decreases but Does Not Eliminate Beliefs in Neuromyths." *Frontiers in Psychology* 8(1314).

OECD (Organisation for Economic Co-operation and Development). 2002. *Understanding the Brain: Towards a New Learning Science.* Paris: OECD.

Salas, E., S.I. Tannenbaum, K. Kraiger, and K.A. Smith-Jentsch. 2012. "The Science of Training and Development in Organizations: What Matters in Practice." *Psychological Science in the Public Interest* 13(2): 74-101.

Shank, P. 2016. *The Science of Learning.* Alexandria, VA: ATD Press.

Useful Websites

- **ATD Science of Learning Content Area:** www.td.org/topics/science-of-learning
- **Daniel Willingham's Science and Education Blog:** www.danielwillingham.com/daniel-willingham-science-and-education-blog
- **The Debunker Club:** www.debunker.club
- **Mirjam Neelen's 3-Star Learning Experiences Blog:** www.3starlearningexperiences.wordpress.com
- **Neurobollocks Blog:** www.neurobollocks.wordpress.com
- **Carnegie Mellon University's LearnLab:** www.learnlab.org
- **The Serious eLearning Manifesto:** www.elearningmanifesto.org
- **Will Thalheimer's Work-Learning Research Blog:** www.worklearning.com
- **Will Thalheimer's Research Library:** www.worklearning.com/catalog

MYTHBUSTERS

Several leaders in the field have taken the science of learning and put it into practice for workplace learning. Beyond the academics that perform learning science research, there are those who also research the implications for instructional design and workplace learning.

I want to take a minute to recognize the stalwarts who do this on an independent basis. These people, some of whom I've mentioned throughout the book, are worth tracking for their insights.

My colleague Will Thalheimer has been a fervent crusader against myths. He regularly reads learning journals, and documents the important outcomes for practice through Work-Learning Research. He has personally been part of the effort to quash Dale's Cone, for example, and put his own money up to anyone who could demonstrate the validity of learning styles. It's been a number of years since he put out his offer about learning styles, but there're still no takers! He also created the Debunker Club (www.debunker .club), where you can join like-minded professionals on smashing myths.

Patti Shank led the eLearning Guild's research, and writes regularly for ATD's Science of Learning blog. Through Learning Peaks, she's another who researches what science has to say to practice. Her new series of books, *Make It Learnable,* provide a distillation of research principles for practice.

Ruth Clark has been lead author on a couple of important books about the science of learning. *eLearning and the Science of Instruction,* co-authored with Richard Mayer of UCSB, presented Mayer and John Sweller's research on multimedia and learning. *Efficiency in Learning,* co-authored with Frank

Nguyen and John Sweller, pulled together a broader suite of research beyond just e-learning, based on Sweller's work under the cognitive load umbrella.

Other avid debunkers who puncture silliness and myths in learning include Julie Dirksen (author of *Design for How People Learn*) and Michael Allen (author of numerous books, including *Michael Allen's Guide to eLearning*), who are also both instigators of the Serious eLearning Manifesto with Will and myself. Donald Clark (both of them, although very differently) and Guy Wallace also pay attention and call out problems. Roger Schank and Allison Rossett have transcended the academic life, but still make the call for good learning. And Mirjam Neelen partners with Paul Kirschner on the 3-Star Learning Experiences blog. I'm sure there are more I'm forgetting. Mea culpa.

Speaking of Paul Kirschner, I would be remiss if I didn't mention De Bruyckere, Kirschner, and Hulshof's *Urban Myths About Learning and Education*. This book similarly unpacks myths, with more of an education focus (including a whole section on education policy), whereas here I'm focused on workplace learning. While there's some overlap, they're covering some things I'm not, and vice-versa. Also, and after all the disclaimers about science, I will admit that I disagree with them on some of their assessments.

ABOUT THE AUTHOR

 Clark Quinn, PhD, has been on the cutting edge of technology and learning since designing his own major on computer-based education as an undergraduate. As part of that process, he was a researcher on a project on conducting learning discussion via email in 1979(!). Making e-learning his career, he's developed an international reputation as an expert, both as a scholar and presenter, as well as a highly regarded consultant providing strategic solutions to Fortune 500, education, government, and not-for-profit organizations. He works for clients as executive director of Quinnovation, and is affiliated with the Internet Time Alliance and Change Agents WorldWide.

Clark designed and programmed educational computer games for DesignWare after college, establishing a theme that has recurred throughout his career. Continuing projects integrating practice and theory on games and learning ultimately led to his book, *Engaging Learning: Designing e-Learning Simulation Games*. He's continued to write about games, run workshops on how to design them, and, of course, design them. Design is a recurrent theme, and Clark's focus on engagement has led to articles and presentations on the role of emotion in learning, as well as consulting on improvements to traditional instructional design.

Clark's also become an acknowledged expert in mobile learning, writing an article in 2000 that has subsequently led to solutions, research, and projects and, most recently, the books *Designing mLearning: Tapping into the Mobile Revolution for Organizational Performance* and *The Mobile Academy: mLearning for Higher Education*. He regularly writes and talks about mobile design, and consults on mobile strategy.

Prior to establishing Quinnovation, Clark headed research and development efforts for Knowledge Universe Interactive Studio, and held management positions at Open Net and Access CMC, two Australian initiatives in Internet-based multimedia and education. He has also held academic positions at the University of New South Wales, the University of Pittsburgh's Learning Research and Development Center, and San Diego State University's Center for Research in Mathematics and Science Education.

Clark's been recognized for his leadership in the design of learning technology through invitations to speak nationally and internationally, as well as being chosen as the eLearning Guild's first *Guild Master* in 2012. As part of his work, he's seen the need for a focus above the individual tactics. Organizations are increasingly looking for strategic guidance in leveraging technology across the organization to facilitate innovation, and Clark's unique combination of creativity with practicality has led him to continue to develop useful models to create e-learning road maps. His vision for learning technology strategy was captured in his book *Revolutionize Learning & Development: Performance and Innovation Strategy for the Information Age*. With a deep understanding of how we learn, broad experience with technology, and solid grounding in business, Clark has a proven ability to develop innovative approaches and deliver them pragmatically as successful solutions.

QUICK GUIDES TO THE MYTHS

10 PERCENT OF OUR BRAIN

CLAIM	Humans use only 10 percent of their brain.
RESEARCH METHOD	Brain scans.
BASIS	Boyd, R. 2008. "Do People Only Use 10% of Their Brains?" *Scientific American,* February 8. www.scientificamerican. com/article/do-people-only-use-10-percent-of-their -brains.
STATUS	We use our entire brain, just at different times.
COMMENTS	» We can improve our thinking, but through learning. » Our brains operate in distributed ways, so it may appear that parts are not being used.
RECOMMENDATION	Develop your skills through practice.

ATTENTION SPAN OF A GOLDFISH

CLAIM	Humans have changed to having the attention span of a goldfish.
RESEARCH METHOD	Research on attention.
BASIS	Shank, P. 2017. *Attention and the 8-Second Span*. eLearning Industry, April 4. https://elearningindustry.com/ 8-second-attention-span-organizational-learning.
STATUS	Our attention hasn't changed; we can still choose to pay attention to something for as long as we want.
COMMENTS	» We can follow movies or games for hours! » Although we can attend, don't assume we will. » The original data purportedly came from Microsoft Canada research, but investigation reveals it's a misinterpretation.
RECOMMENDATION	Design to acquire and maintain attention.

BRAIN TRAINING

CLAIM	Regular brain-training activities can improve mental reasoning.
RESEARCH METHOD	Meta-analysis.
BASIS	Simons, D.J., W.R. Boot, N. Charness, S.E. Gathercole, C.F. Chabris, D.Z. Hambrick, and E.A. Stine-Morrow. 2016. "Do 'Brain-Training' Programs Work?" *Psychological Science in the Public Interest* 17(3): 103-186.
STATUS	There is no evidence that brain training helps general functioning.
COMMENTS	» May prevent cognitive deterioration as we age. » Training doesn't transfer well. » There's a difference between studies suppliers show you and what science requires.
RECOMMENDATION	Train for what you want to be able to do.

DALE'S CONE

CLAIM	People remember 10 percent of what they read and 90 percent of what they do.
RESEARCH METHOD	Historical investigation.
BASIS	Subramony, D., M. Molenda, A. Betrus, and W. Thalheimer. 2014. "The Mythical Retention Chart and the Corruption of Dale's Cone of Experience." *Educational Technology* 54(6): 6-16.
STATUS	A case study of appropriation without sufficient diligence.
COMMENTS	» The original cone didn't have numbers. » The current numbers are too perfect to be real. » The story clearly demonstrates the need to be careful in circulating or believing presented data.
RECOMMENDATION	Do design for practice, and do consider the appropriate use of media. However, do the diligence to determine sufficient *and* appropriate practice and media.

DIGITAL MEANS WE LEARN DIFFERENTLY

CLAIM	New technology behaviors mean we'll learn differently.
RESEARCH METHOD	An evolutionary argument.
BASIS	Brandon, R.N., and N. Hornstein. 1986. "From Icons to Symbols: Some Speculations on the Origins of Language." *Biology and Philosophy* 1:169-189.
STATUS	The timescale of brain evolution is much, much slower than the rate of digital change.
COMMENTS	» We might use technology differently to learn, but what it means to learn remains the same. » We should use technology to enhance learning. » We still need to align with our brain's architecture.
RECOMMENDATION	Stick to what's known about creating real learning: design spaced, meaningful practice and complement with guided reflection.

DIGITAL NATIVES

CLAIM	Those who grew up in the digital age have unique skills with technology.
RESEARCH METHOD	Research surveys.
BASIS	Jones, C., and B. Shao. 2011. "The Net Generation and Digital Natives: Implications for Higher Education." New York: Higher Education Academy.
STATUS	Youth who grew up with technology do not possess specific abilities.
COMMENTS	» Youth who grew up with technology may be more comfortable with technology. » The data do not show that those who grow up with technology have more comprehensive skills. » This would be a mild form of discrimination.
RECOMMENDATION	Assess and address individual skills with technology, don't assume or characterize on another basis.

ERROR-FREE LEARNING

CLAIM	Making mistakes is not useful for learning.
RESEARCH METHOD	Research review.
BASIS	Metcalfe, J. 2017. "Learning From Errors." *Annual Review of Psychology* 68.
STATUS	Errors, with appropriate feedback, are valuable for learning.
COMMENTS	» Mistakes are OK. » Learners need good feedback. » The best alternatives to the right answer are common mistakes. » Learning from mistakes is a valuable skill on its own.
RECOMMENDATION	Design an appropriate challenge into your practice problems. Mistakes should be possible, but provide good feedback and make it safe to fail.

GENERATIONS

CLAIM	Individual workplace values can be characterized by the era people grew up in.
RESEARCH METHOD	Surveys of different generations.
BASIS	Lester, S.W., R.L. Standifer, N.J. Schultz, and J.M. Windsor. 2012. "Actual Versus Perceived Generational Differences at Work: An Empirical Examination." *Journal of Leadership & Organizational Studies* 19:341-354. Mencl, J., and S.W. Lester. 2014. "More Alike Than Different: What Generations Value and How the Values Affect Employee Workplace Perceptions." *Journal of Leadership & Organizational Studies* 21(3): 257-272.
STATUS	Not significantly different.
COMMENTS	» The differences between individual circumstances have more impact than social contexts people grew up with. » It's likely that those environments aren't fundamentally linked. » This is a form of discrimination.
RECOMMENDATION	Design learning for people by their individual behaviors, not the date of their birth.

IMAGES ARE 60,000 TIMES BETTER THAN TEXT

CLAIM	People process images 60,000 times faster than text.
RESEARCH METHOD	Search for original claim.
BASIS	Levine, A. 2016. "Stop the Madness: The Proliferation of the 60000 Times Faster Myth Dances On." Cog Dog Blog, May 1. http://cogdogblog.com/2016/05/stop-the-madness.
STATUS	No evidence.
COMMENTS	» Images and text are visual. » Either may require processing or benefit from recognition.
RECOMMENDATION	Use the right media for the cognitive role.

LEARNING STYLES: ADAPTATION

CLAIM	We should adapt learning to learners based on their learning style.
RESEARCH METHOD	A research survey was conducted across a number of studies.
BASIS	Pashler, H., M. McDaniel, D. Rohrer, and R. Bjork. 2008. "Learning Styles: Concepts and Evidence." *Psychological Science in the Public Interest* 9(3): 105-119.
STATUS	There is no evidence that adapting to learning styles benefits the learning outcome.
COMMENTS	» There are good bases for adapting learning. » However, learning styles isn't one. » This isn't to say that it won't change, but it's the way to bet for now.
RECOMMENDATION	Adapt content to the learner's recent performance, preferences, roles, or experience.

LEARNING STYLES: MEASUREMENT

CLAIM	We can reliably categorize individuals by their learning styles.
RESEARCH METHOD	An evaluation of a representative sample of learning styles instruments—including Myers–Briggs and Kolb—was conducted on four core measures of psychometric validity.
BASIS	Coffield, F., D. Mosely, E. Hall, and K. Ecclestone. 2004. *Should We Be Using Learning Styles? What Research Has to Say to Practice.* London: Learning & Skills Research Centre.
STATUS	The researchers found just one measure, a one-dimensional instrument of limited utility, that met all four standards. None of the others did. They cited reasons such as proprietary instruments that had little motivation to publicize their research.
COMMENTS	» This result suggests that only open and widely shared data are likely to have a solid foundation. There is no reason to believe in any proprietary instrument. » The OCEAN instrument (the "Big 5"), which is being developed as a shared initiative by personality psychometricians, has the best hope of being a legitimate personality assessment. » Of the instruments studied, the two that hold the most promise as learning style instruments are those by Vermunt and Entwistle, which are both open research exercises. » This isn't to say that there won't ultimately be a valid instrument, but current challenges include the variability by learning goal, and context for learning.
RECOMMENDATION	Design for the learning goal, not the learner.

LEFT AND RIGHT BRAIN

CLAIM	People can be characterized by their relative proportion of left or right brain capabilities.
RESEARCH METHOD	Brain imaging.
BASIS	Nielsen, J.A., B.A. Zielinski, M.A. Ferguson, J.E. Lainhart, and J.S. Anderson. 2013. "An Evaluation of the Left-Brain vs. Right-Brain Hypothesis With Resting State Functional Connectivity Magnetic Resonance Imaging." *PLoS ONE* 8(8).
STATUS	While there are some differing functions in the brain's hemispheres, there isn't a valid basis to characterize people or adapt learning.
COMMENTS	This is similar to the learning styles myth.
RECOMMENDATION	Design for what needs to be learned, and characterize people by their behaviors.

MALE AND FEMALE DIFFERENCES IN LEARNING

CLAIM	Brain differences between men and women mean we need to design learning differently for each.
RESEARCH METHOD	Brain scans.
BASIS	Joel, D., Z. Berman, I. Tavor, N. Wexler, O. Gaber, Y. Stein, N. Shefi, J. Pool, S. Urchs, D.S. Margulies, F. Liem, J. Hanggi, L. Jancke, and Y. Assif. 2015. "Sex Beyond the Genitalia: The Human Brain Mosaic." *Proceedings of the National Academy of Sciences* 112(50).
STATUS	The differences are so variable as to not be a good basis.
COMMENTS	» Use the best learning design. » This also holds true for workplace practices.
RECOMMENDATION	Design for the learning, not the learner.

MULTITASKING

CLAIM	We can effectively multitask across a number of attention-requiring actions.
RESEARCH METHOD	Cognitive assessment.
BASIS	American Psychological Association. 2006. "Multi-tasking: Switching Costs." www.apa.org/research/action/multitask.aspx.
STATUS	We are slower or less effective when we multitask.
COMMENTS	» Multitasking depends very heavily on the degree to which the tasks are automated. » We'll likely make more mistakes and take longer on component tasks if we multitask.
RECOMMENDATION	Minimize multitasking requirements by managing cognitive load through practice or support.

NEURO-LINGUISTIC PROGRAMMING

CLAIM	We can improve our behavior through neuro-linguistic programming initiatives based upon language and action.
RESEARCH METHOD	Research survey.
BASIS	Witkowski, T. 2011. "Thirty-Five Years of Research on Neuro-Linguistic Programming. NLP Research Data Base. State of the Art or Pseudoscientific Decoration?" *Polish Psychological Bulletin* 41(2): 58-66.
STATUS	The neuro-linguistic programming approach fails on both empirical and conceptual grounds.
COMMENTS	» Cognitive behavioral therapy is a research-based personal improvement approach, whereas neuro-linguistic programming lacks scientific support. » Use training to develop specific behavior responses.
RECOMMENDATION	Use appropriate learning design when you want a group to develop specific behavioral skills.

PEOPLE DON'T NEED KNOWLEDGE

CLAIM	People don't need knowledge, only skills.
RESEARCH METHOD	Research survey.
BASIS	Willingham, D.T. 2006. "How Knowledge Helps: It Speeds and Strengthens Reading Comprehension, Learning—and Thinking." *American Educator* 1:30.
STATUS	Knowledge plays a critical role in the ability to apply skills appropriately.
COMMENTS	» You want the minimum knowledge. » But you do need it.
RECOMMENDATION	Be careful to winnow knowledge down to the essential, and then focus on knowledge to develop skills. Neither alone is sufficient.

QUICK GUIDES TO THE SUPERSTITIONS

INTERACTION = ENGAGEMENT

CLAIM	Interactions like clicking are intrinsically interesting.
RATIONALE	Clicking makes the experience more active, and consequently more engaging.
WHY NOT	Gratuitous clicking that doesn't have an emotional or cognitive payoff isn't really engaging, and neither is just revealing more content.
COMMENTS	» Clicking to see more is just a trick to present more content! » Learners don't want more content. » Challenge is engaging: have them make meaningful distinctions.
ALTERNATIVE	Have learners make a choice and then see the consequences.

KNOWLEDGE TEST = LEARNING OUTCOME

CLAIM	If they can recite it, they can do it.
RATIONALE	It's easy, and looks like learning we know.
WHY NOT	Unless recitation is our need (and rarely is it or should it be), you need to apply the knowledge like it needs to be applied in the performance situation.
COMMENTS	» It can be better-written multiple-choice questions. » Simulations or branching scenarios are better. » It should be multiple practices of the same thing, over time.
ALTERNATIVE	Design practice that requires the learners to make decisions like they'll need to make in the workplace.

LEARNING SHOULD BE EASY OR HARD

CLAIM	Learning needs to be either really hard (to actually work) or really easy (so learners don't feel bad).
RATIONALE	Learning should be either fun or tough.
WHY NOT	Learning happens best when the learner is neither bored nor frustrated, so you want to adjust the challenge to the capability of the learner.
COMMENTS	» Too easy is boring. » Too hard is frustrating. » Some challenge is just right. » Learning can, and should, be hard fun.
ALTERNATIVE	Make the alternatives to the right answer be reliable ways learners go wrong, and make the discrimination more difficult at the learner's pace until they can make those decisions at the necessary level.

PRESENTATION = ACQUISITION

CLAIM	If you've covered it, they've learned it.
RATIONALE	They will remember it and can infer how to use it.
WHY NOT	To be retained, information needs multiple exposures and actual retrieval practice. For it to be used, it needs to be retrieved and applied.
COMMENTS	» This applies to microlearning that's just a single overall course broken down into smaller segments; one presentation isn't likely to be there later. » The spacing effect is relevant here, as is the forgetting curve. » Even telling learners multiple times is unlikely to be useful.
ALTERNATIVE	Design learning to require retrieval and application of content in context. Multiple times.

SMILE SHEETS = EVALUATION

CLAIM	If they like it, it is effective.
RATIONALE	Level 1 evaluation is at least some evaluation.
WHY NOT	People's opinions of the learnings don't correlate with the real impact.
COMMENTS	» You should start with the change that needs to happen. » You should figure out what people need to do differently, then you should design learning to impact that. » Ultimately, test whether the learning is leading to behavior change and a business impact. » Only then should you measure whether people find it engaging.
ALTERNATIVE	Measure the outcomes of the learning, changes in workplace behavior, and the impact on metrics that need to change.

QUICK GUIDES TO THE MISCONCEPTIONS

70-20-10

CLAIM	It's a useful framework for thinking about achieving outcomes.
COUNTER	The numbers aren't research-based.
RECONCILIATION	It's not about the numbers, it's about the outcomes.
COMMENTS	» It may have benefited from a different label. » There was research that justified similar numbers. » The numbers aren't exact. » It's about achieving real outcomes.
RECOMMENDATION	Find out what 70-20-10 is, and use it if it's useful to you.

7-38-55

CLAIM	Communication is 7 percent words, 38 percent tone, and 55 percent body language.
COUNTER	That seems contrary to most of what we know.
RECONCILIATION	The data that generated this were only for situations where you have no other knowledge, and are only talking about subjective experience.
COMMENTS	» This is another example of over-extending data.
RECOMMENDATION	Be aware of all aspects of communication—including what you know about the person, what you say, and how you say it—but in general you can infer that what you say will have a substantial impact.

BLOOM'S TAXONOMY

CLAIM	Bloom's Taxonomy is a useful guide for designing learning.
COUNTER	It is overly complex and not aligned with learning science.
RECONCILIATION	Bloom's Taxonomy can be simplified into a more useful form.
COMMENTS	» What decisions do the learners need to be able to make? » What knowledge do learners need to be able to make those decisions? » What else do you need?
RECOMMENDATION	Focus on what the learners need to do, and the knowledge they need to be able to do it.

BRAINSTORMING

CLAIM	Brainstorming doesn't work.
COUNTER	We get better results when we apply multiple brains.
RECONCILIATION	Allowing individual work before group work prevents groupthink.
COMMENTS	» Individuals need to ideate alone before group work. » The group work needs to be facilitated to make it safe and equal. » Nature and timeouts facilitate idea incubation.
RECOMMENDATION	Figure out how to do brainstorming, then do it!

THE EXPERIENCE API

CLAIM	xAPI is an important step beyond course tracking.
COUNTER	Not all that matters can be measured.
RECONCILIATION	While not a panacea, there is value in xAPI because it can collect data that can be collated with business intelligence.
COMMENTS	» Think about what data would be useful. » Look for your vendors to incorporate xAPI. » Think about what data the business has that can be correlated with the data collected by xAPI. » Think: measurement!
RECOMMENDATION	Start preparing to use xAPI (or equivalent) if you aren't already.

GAMIFICATION

CLAIM	Gamification is a valuable contribution to achieving learning outcomes.
COUNTER	Gamification appeals to extrinsic interest, but intrinsic interest is superior.
RECONCILIATION	Both have their roles: Intrinsic interest is superior, but gamification can add additional motivation.
COMMENTS	» Be very careful about what you reward with points. » SMEs have studied the topic you're training on for some reason—find it and use it! » At a minimum, rewrite knowledge questions as mini-scenarios; make learners use the information.
RECOMMENDATION	Get the intrinsic interest in there first. Then follow up with gamification where useful.

HUMOR IN LEARNING

CLAIM	Avoid using humor in learning.
COUNTER	Humor can build community, relax learners, and make learning stick better.
RECONCILIATION	The issue is not whether to use humor, but when and how.
COMMENTS	» Humor shouldn't overwhelm the message. » Humor can lighten the mood. » Humor can build community. » Humor can make learning stick better.
RECOMMENDATION	Use humor appropriately: positively, not too frequently, and to make the learning point.

KIRKPATRICK MODEL OF EVALUATION

CLAIM	The Kirkpatrick model isn't an effective evaluation model.
COUNTER	It's not designed to be a learning evaluation model, it's a business impact evaluation.
RECONCILIATION	It's not being used right, but is useful as a design tool.
COMMENTS	» It can be used for more than training. » Level 1 isn't of much use. » You can use other tools for Level 2.
RECOMMENDATION	Use Kirkpatrick to guide your design: Start with Level 4, and work through 3 down to 2, then back up again once you've implemented. It's a way to validate that you're having an impact.

LEARNING MANAGEMENT SYSTEMS

CLAIM	A learning management system is the key software to support L&D.
COUNTER	We're beyond a course-centric view of L&D.
RECONCILIATION	Courses are still part of L&D, but only one part.
COMMENTS	» You can't "manage" learning. » Think about the extended learning experience, not courses. » A performer-centric view looks at performance support resources, communication and collaboration, and individual curation and creation.
RECOMMENDATION	Adopt a performance ecosystem perspective.

META-LEARNING

CLAIM	There are no domain-independent learning skills.
COUNTER	Research has identified a number of effective learning skills.
RECONCILIATION	Domain-specific skills are more powerful, but the value of domain-independent skills will likely increase.
COMMENTS	» Highlighting and underlining aren't valuable. » Note-taking requires some specifics to be effective. » Self-explanation, interleaved practice, and elaborative interrogation can have value. » Knowing how to do something effectively is valuable.
RECOMMENDATION	Assess and develop meta-learning skills, don't take them for granted.

MICROLEARNING

CLAIM	Microlearning, small bits of content, is the solution to learning.
COUNTER	There's a confound between performance support and learning on the one hand, and on the other there are unexamined nuances in actually making the learning side work.
RECONCILIATION	Performance support is preferred, but if you want to do the training, know the details to make it actually stick.
COMMENTS	» While testing is best, even estimates of retention can be used. » Showing "how to" doesn't need to lead to learning if it gets the job done.
RECOMMENDATION	Use performance support when you can, and use the details to make training actually work.

mLearning

CLAIM	Any learning through a mobile device is mlearning.
COUNTER	Mobile learning can be much more, such as providing performance support.
RECONCILIATION	Mobile learning should be both.
COMMENTS	» Performance support is mobile's sweet spot. » Social learning is a natural use of mobile devices. » Mobile also is a great way to augment formal learning. » Supporting people whenever and wherever they are is valuable. » The unique opportunity is doing things when and where they are.
RECOMMENDATION	Look at mobile as a platform, and consider the full suite of possible uses, including augmenting learning, performance support, social learning, and contextual support.

NeuroX or BrainX

CLAIM	NeuroX or BrainX (where X = learning, leadership, -based, and so on) has important lessons.
COUNTER	The findings that influence practice come from the broader field of cognitive science.
RECONCILIATION	The valuable lessons about what we should do and how come from cognitive and learning sciences; the neural explanations largely explain why.
COMMENTS	» "The neurons that fire together, wire together" is about as much neural knowledge as you need. » The emotional side of learning is valuable, but that's known.
RECOMMENDATION	Be an informed consumer: know the brain basics, and scrutinize claims with a skeptical eye.

PROBLEM-BASED LEARNING

CLAIM	Problem-based learning naturally integrates interest and leads to better outcomes.
COUNTER	Direct instruction is the best approach.
RECONCILIATION	It depends on the outcome and definitions, but for long-term retention and transfer, problem-based learning is the best option.
COMMENTS	» Problem-based learning must be guided, not just pure discovery. » PBL does not stand for points, badges, and leaderboards.
RECOMMENDATION	Make your learning problem-based at least by having meaningful problems.

SOCIAL LEARNING

CLAIM	Social learning is hype.
COUNTER	We naturally learn socially.
RECONCILIATION	The issue is when to include social activities.
COMMENTS	» Negotiating a shared understanding is both engaging and valuable. » Social makes sense when the topic is complex. » Coaching after the learning experience is a powerful ally. » Don't assume social learning skills, develop and assess them.
RECOMMENDATION	Use social learning to enrich understanding when the task is more complex or further transfer is needed.

UNLEARNING

CLAIM	The key skill in an era of increasing change is the ability to unlearn.
COUNTER	There is no cognitive mechanism for unlearning.
RECONCILIATION	Unlearning is just learning over the old memory traces.
COMMENTS	» Try not to have people learn volatile information. » Recognize that overlearning takes time, and it can be easy to slide back into old habits.
RECOMMENDATION	Don't make people learn something that can be accessed easily. When people must learn, be prepared to provide sufficient practice to assure success.